OGDOA

OGDOADIC MAGICK

Being a Year of Study
With an Aurum Solis Commandery

Norman R. Kraft

WEISER BOOKS
Boston, MA/York Beach, ME

First published in 2001 by
Red Wheel/Weiser, LLC
P. O. Box 612
York Beach, ME 03910-0612

Library of Congress Cataloging-in-Publication Data
Kraft, Norman R.
    Ogdoadic magick: being a year of study with an Aurum solis
commandery/Norman R. Kraft
        p. cm.
    Includes bibliographical references and index.
    ISBN 1-57863-208-0 (pbk.: alk. paper)
    1. Magic. I. Title
BF1611 .K69 2001
135'.4—dc21   2001017719

Typeset in Giovanni Book
TCP

Cover art is *The Annunciation.* Reproduction by permission of the Syndies of the
Fitzwilliam Museum, Cambridge. This painting is the work of an unknown 16th-
century artist from the Flemish school. It is an excellent example of the use of
symbolism in works of devotional art, containing a rich mixture of religious, geometric and pagan symbols, many of which will be quite familiar to those who
practice Aurum Solis Magick. The painting has an honored place in the greater
Ogdoadic tradition and is used as a teaching tool in the Aurum Solis for students
at the intermediate level.

For a list of quoted text permissions see Acknowledgments on page xiv.

Printed in Canada

08 07 06 05 04 03 02 01
8   7   6   5   4   3   2   1

The paper used in this publication meets the minimum requirements of the
American National Standard for Information Sciences—Permanence of Paper for
Printed Library Materials Z39.48-1992 (R1997).

DEDICATION

To my mother, who inspired my journeys and taught us to
look to the stars. May she dance ever among them.

This book is dedicated to all those who aspire to the
splendor of the Star which unites us.

CONTENTS

LIST OF RITUALS

ACKNOWLEDGMENTS

I extend my grateful thanks to the following, in the full knowledge that, without their participation, this book would never have happened:

To the Artisans of Lapis Lazuli, who were instrumental in testing this material. I will always feel deeply honored to have worked with you for so long.

To those who read various chapters and early drafts of this book: Sarah, Peter, Silvia, Jeanie, John, Jim, and David. Thank you all for taking the time to read and comment upon this text while I was pulling its various parts together.

To Leon Barcynski, Grand Master of the Aurum Solis Order, for his inspiration and tireless efforts on behalf of the order, and for his gracious permission to quote widely from previously unpublished Aurum Solis material.

To Jeanie Marie Mossa, my wife and the talented artist behind many of the illustrations in this book, which appear here with her gracious permission. Her infinite patience, understanding, love and support made this book, and my life, possible.

For permission to use copyright material, I gratefully make the following acknowledgments:

Llewellyn Worldwide, Ltd. for permission to use Aurum Solis document quotations from *The Magical Philosophy*, Revised Edition Volume I: *Foundations of High Magick* by Denning & Phillips © 1992, Volume II: *The Sword and the Serpent* by Denning and Phillips © 1998, Volume III: *Mysteria Magica* by Denning & Phillips © 1988 and *Planetary Magick*, First Edition by Denning & Phillips ©1989. All published by Llewellyn Worldwide, Ltd. P.O. Box 64383, St. Paul, MN 55164. All rights reserved.

Harcourt, Inc. for permission to use the excerpt on page 10 from "Choruses From The Rock" in *Collected Poems*1909–1962 by T. S. Eliot, copyright © 1936 by Harcourt, Inc., copyright © 1964, 1963 by T. S. Eliot.

Please note product may ship from multiple locations and may arrive in separate packages at different times.

Return Policy:

All items purchased through goHastings may be returned for a full refund of the purchase price. All items must be in original unopened packaging, and returned within 30 days of when it was shipped. Shipping and handling charges are not refundable. For full refund details please contact Customer Service at (877) – HASTINGS.

Thank You for shopping with goHastings on Amazon.com

Pick ID: 1

Assoc ID: 32083

Page 1 of 1

Customer Service: (877) – HASTINGS (427–8464)
E-mail: service@goHastings.com
Return Address: Hastings Entertainment
3601 Plains Blvd
Amarillo, TX 79102

Order Number: 116–8736127–5566643 18681781

Ship Date: 03/24/2016
Buyer Name: JOSEPH A KLEEHAMMER
Seller Name: goHastings

Shipping Address:
JOSEPH A KLEEHAMMER
516 BAVERTON LN

HASLET TX, 76052

Title	USED – OGDOADIC MAGICK	
Web–Title	OGDOADIC MAGICK : BEING A YEAR OF S	
Artist	KRAFT, NORMAN R	
Department	BOOKS	Street Date: 07/31/2001
Category	RELIGION	N/A
Format	TRADE PAPERBACK	N/A

Standard Shipping

Used barcode: 40018753135
New barcode: 1578632080
Product Format: USED

Ship QTY	1
On hand	1
fixture #	N/A
Last received	02/14/2016
SSP	9619001099
Promo	

FOREWORD

To be convinced of the reality of magical power—that is, of an invisible force capable of producing a designated effect upon a living person or upon an inanimate object—is not difficult if we approach the abundant and well-attested evidence without prejudice, and without regard to the scientific device of naming phenomena. Telepathy, hypnotism, psychic healing, psychokinesis, out-of-body experiences, precognition, psychometry—the existence of these skills and of other techniques for winning knowledge or exerting influence is widely recognized in the world today.

The inquirer can examine the evidence and be assured of the reality of the above-mentioned skills and techniques by accepting the verdict of their senses and their reason. One need not have, in other words, any particular faith in God or humankind, nor even in self in order to realize they exist. Beyond this initial tempering of scepticism, however, the mere knowledge of the existence of magical power is not likely to be of much service to the inquirer.

To make a real and lasting progress in the magical art requires much more. The aspirant needs to have a kind of "faith," which is not the nebulous or pietistic optimism that frequently goes by that name. Real faith is impossible without knowledge: you must not only understand how to climb your rope ladder, you need to know for a certainty that the top is firmly fixed, and fixed where you want it, before you start from the bottom. So, too, the traveler upon an unknown road requires a reliable map and compass. This perception is much to the point in the beginning made in *Ogdoadic Magick*.

The aspirant's mystical map of ascent, as Norman Kraft succinctly indicates, is the Qabalistic Tree of Life, which can also be understood as the plan of his or her psycho-spiritual being—body, soul and spirit. And the Tree of Life is, from the outset, complete and entire within the psyche as the aspirant's birthright, if as yet awaiting his or her inner discovery.

Sometimes a taunt is raised against the way of High Magick, to the effect that it is directed solely toward remote mystical attainment. This criticism only shows a lack of understanding of the necessary cause and effect. To develop and direct the relevant faculties of the physical body and of the astral and mental levels of the psyche, as well as finding awareness of true spiritual values—and to bring all these matters into co-ordination—will undoubtedly, in the long course of events, bring the aspirant to the mystical heights. But upon that long road the aspirant utilizes this same training in order to bring the abilities and skills of the magician to dynamic potency within the psyche.

In *Ogdoadic Magick*, Norman Kraft skillfully guides the aspirant through the early stages of magical development, to establish a true and potent interaction of the natural faculties of the body and the astral levels of the psyche with the external pulses of the cosmos. The task, acknowledged here, is not laboriously to bring into existence the forces with which the magician operates; it is to recognize their existing reality, to know them reverently, and to direct them aright.

—Osborne Phillips *i.e. "PHILLIPS & DENNING"*

INTRODUCTION

Each soul is potentially divine. The goal is to manifest
this divinity within by controlling nature, external and
internal. Do this either by work, worship, psychic control or philosophy—by one, or more, or all of these—
and be free. This is the whole of religion. Doctrines,
dogmas, rituals, books, temples, and forms, are but sec-
ondary details.[1]

As Master of the Commandery of the Black Rose of the Order
Aurum Solis (and former Master of the Lapis Lazuli
Commandery), I meet many people who have an interest in the
Art Magick of our great tradition. Ours is a small order, however,
and oriented toward group work for those living in close proxim-
ity to one another. It accepts new members on an invitation-only
basis. Thus, many of those who wish to learn the Aurum Solis system do so on their own. For many, geography prevents group study
with an existing Commandery. Circumstance dictates that they follow the path of the solitary magician. Others simply prefer the

path of the solitary magician, without seeking ties or involvement in the group activities of a magical order. Yet even those who may have the determination, creativity and persistence necessary to pursue this system without group support and direction are often frustrated to find that the core books of the public portions of the Aurum Solis tradition are often difficult to obtain. In addition, books about Aurum Solis with beginners in mind have been virtually non-existent.

This book was written with the solitary practitioner in mind and assumes you have no background in Magick. It encompasses roughly one year's worth of practice and study. In its earliest form, this text was a three page outline showing the new members at Lapis Lazuli Commandery the work that was anticipated in the course of their first year of study. Over the years I expanded upon this document, answered many questions about it, worked through difficult passages, and incorporated more Order material (with permission of the Order, of course). The final result is this book and another intermediate text yet to be published.

From its inception, Aurum Solis has been based, not on Rosicrucianism or Freemasonry, but around Gnostic, Greek, Celtic, and alchemical philosophies and practices, and this is what has drawn many to the Order. Further, Aurum Solis is steeped in Qabalah, but a Qabalah of different traditions and lineage than those used by the Golden Dawn. Its desire and purpose has been to detach the timeless teachings of the Qabalah from the limitations of historical and theological considerations and restate them for the modern student of high magick.

If you, the reader, devote one year to this study and exploration of the Aurum Solis magical current, I can promise that you will learn a great deal about magick and about Aurum Solis. Most of all you will learn about life. For magick is about life and light, and discovery of the true self. The study of magick can never take place apart from the study of life. This book will show you the basic tools of magick and some characteristic workings of the Aurum Solis Ogdoadic tradition. Your task is to apply these tools to your own life, and through them to change and mold your world.

Before we take that first step together, however, I ask you to look within and give some serious thought to this question we ask all new initiates to the Aurum Solis First Hall:

Child of Earth and Starry Heaven, thou who seekest this day the experience of the Mysteries, who seekest a clearer vision of Truth; thou who seekest worlds within worlds until for thee all worlds are one in eternity; the High Company of the Glorious Star greets thee.

Before we proceed, know this: Whoso enters the Mysteries can nevermore return to the evening world of unenlightened selfhood. To take the first step upon the Sacred Way of Return is to be committed to it forever. To enter upon this path is to find New Life in the morning world of Divine Inspiration, until all shall be caught up and assumed into the transforming Fire of Godhead.

I ask thee most seriously, therefore, art thou determined to make this venture and to undergo this transformation?[2]

Are you ready and determined to explore your true potential? If so, turn the page and let us begin!

1

WHAT IS MAGICK?

Tere are many beautiful or popular definitions of magick. Denning and Phillips, noted authors in the Aurum Solis tradition, have written that "magick is the production of desired effects, whether in the person of the magician or exterior to it, by means of a deliberate and special use of powers and faculties within the psyche."[1] Murry Hope, a magician of a related tradition defined magick as "concerned with the conversion of universal energies into practical frequencies that can be utilized according to the needs of the occasion. These energies in themselves are totally neutral, having no affiliation with any belief, system or personality either here on Earth or anywhere in the cosmos, their manifestation at the magical level being coloured entirely by the nature and intention of the user."[2] Eliphas Levi beautifully captured the essence of magick when he described it as "...that which God created before all things when He said: Let there be light."[3] Aleister Crowley's definition remains quite popular, though often misunderstood: "magick is the Science and Art of causing Change to occur in conformity with Will."[4]

1

Yet while these quotes have their uses, definitions of magick are akin to definitions of the Tao: by the time you have described it with language, you have already lost contact with it. While many of the tools of magick are those of the mind and intellect, the essence of magick remains mysterious to the intellect, something much more than human, something that exists across realms and modes of being we cannot know from our limited earthly perspective.

While it is natural in the beginning to rely on what other magicians have said about magick, ultimately, magick is something that you will define for yourself. For, in a sense, we all know and feel magick instinctively within ourselves. To read that "every intentional act is a magical act"[5] seems easy enough to grasp, but it begs the question of what we are to do with this information.

In her book *Applied Magic*, Dion Fortune notes that many Eastern systems, such as those of the Tibetans, are quite free in discussing the philosophical and intellectual bases of their systems. It is the practical methods of using that information that remain secret. This is the way of the Western mysteries as well: the Hebrew alphabet and the Qabalistic Tree of Life were once considered deep secrets of sworn brotherhoods, but are now commonly known. While there are many books, Web sites, and classes on these topics, few explore what to *do* with the technologies of the mind and alchemy of spirit discovered through the careful workings of dedicated practitioners. While anyone may grasp the outer forms, the inner mysteries and the secret wisdom of the great magical orders remain as hidden as before.[6]

While much of this question can only be answered much later in the progress of the magician, let us examine a few basic ideas to get started. Magick may be broken down into two primary areas: focus and inspiration. Those two terms can be expanded in many ways: mind and breath, concentration and religious fervor, technique and emotion, etc. It is the focus of will and thought driven by the great power of the light within. *Are ESOTERIC QUAKERS?*

In our culture, focus is the easiest to acquire. We've been taught just about everything in our lives through book learning and memorization. Yet without development in the second area, inspiration, magick goes flat. It is much like a very finely crafted laser device without a light source: lasers merely focus and intensify light that is already there. They cannot create light, no matter how well designed and built they are.

In the West, magick has often suffered from an overdevelopment of its intellectual side. A frequent criticism of Western magicians is that all we do is read and talk, read and talk. While intellect is an important aspect of magick, this emphasis on the mind has contributed to the considerable population of armchair magicians so common today. The study of magick is not like study toward a university degree; it is a way of life and a way of living. One may study medicine, but it is clear to most of us that to become a doctor requires a leap beyond the comprehension of the basic subjects involved.

I have seen many well-designed rituals in which the magicians have performed every detail correctly, yet that simply fall flat in bringing through any kind of real power. No matter how well designed the rite, no matter how brilliant the costumes, wall hangings, and other tools may be, no matter how precisely the magician pronounces each word, these aspects all add up to little more than the finely crafted laser without a light source. Without the inspiration of the heart, without the aspirations that arise from within, the most brilliantly worked rite will not bring through the kind of energy and power we seek.

A magician with drive and inspiration can do more with a poorly crafted rite than a letter-perfect magician who is unenthusiastic about the purpose of the ritual or so distracted by the details that the subtle aspects of the ritual are missed. A poorly designed laser with a bright light source will perform better than the best-built laser with no light. It's as simple as that.

On the other hand, the finely crafted laser with a bright light source will perform better than both of these, generating a powerful, focused beam of energy. And this is what the study and practice of Western magick will develop.

A Magical Theory

How does magick work? Your appreciation of both this question and its answer will change and deepen over time, but allow me to draw on my own background to venture a few thoughts at this point.

Chaos mathematics and systems theory were born of the quest to understand massive, unpredictable processes such as the weather, and, from the lack of a scientific model, to predict something as simple as the path of a column of smoke from an incense stick.

The problem, in each case, is that the smoke and the weather are not "things" at all, but rather integral parts of greater systems of incomprehensible complexity. Thus, as is often said, if a butterfly takes flight from a flowering plant in Japan, its movements have some (if infinitesimally small) effect on the weather in California, and this affects the movements of the column of smoke rising from the incense in your living room. Moreover, we know that our planet and our solar system are inextricably linked with the dance of the galaxy and the movements of other planets and solar systems, and ultimately, with the movements of the galaxy itself as it dances its way with other galaxies in the blackness of space.

We should never consider ourselves as separate from these processes. Every action we take has a measurable effect on our environment and, to some degree, changes the very fabric of our universe. The same is true in reverse: that which changes our universe changes us. Think about this—are you not a very different person on a hot, clear, humid summer day than you are on a frozen and cloudy winter day? This is a large change in environment changing you, but many other smaller changes happen every day, every hour, every moment. Most women are well aware of the subtle but powerful effect the Moon has on their bodies and emotions.

It is a fundamental concept in many philosophical and religious systems that we are complex beings deeply interconnected to and enfolded by our environment and each other. Chinese philosophies such as Taoism are built wholly on this line of thought. As time passes, this basic viewpoint is becoming more a part of Western physics as well.

What has this to do with magick? Imagine, for a moment, our solar system—each planet calmly following its appointed path, the system as a whole calmly moving through the blackness of space. Now, imagine that you reach out and give Mars the tiniest push. That push changes the orbit of Mars around the Sun. It also changes the orbits of the other planets and of the moons that orbit them.

The change to our orbit and our Moon causes a change in the tides here on Earth, which causes a change in the weather, which negatively affects crops in the American Midwest. This changes the price of grain and vegetables in the supermarket, which affects your purchasing patterns, which changes your diet and ultimately impacts your health. (Depending on which direction you pushed Mars, however, such change could be very good for either winter-coat manufacturers or swimsuit designers.)

What has happened is that change has been introduced into the system. This change has made itself felt in the complex inter-actions around it and has altered the entire system. A similar push in another solar system would have quite different effects.

Now imagine that you give Mars just the right push in just the right direction, with maybe a complimentary little push on Venus, and this sets everything back into its normal orbit and movement. Weather and crops are restored to normal, supermarket prices return to normal, and fishermen can once again happily use their tide tables to predict the ebb and flow of the oceans. Harmony is restored.

Magick gives us the tools to effect tiny pushes such as these, affecting both the world around us and the worlds within us in definite, measurable ways. Think of each thing in our universe as spinning in a dance of orbits, big and small. Every person on this Earth is part of that dance, as is every molecule and atom of each cell in each person's body. Each of our movements and each of our decisions changes our universe (spiritual and physical). When these movements and decisions are willed and directed, we call it magick.

Further Thoughts about Magick

These are quotations from other Lapis Lazuli Commandery documents and group discussions that may be of some use to those starting upon the magical way. Some will be revisited later; all are offered as starting points for further thought.

- Magick is not about power, even though you gain power in the course of the work. To hold power as a goal of magick begs the questions: Power over what? Power over whom? If the answer to either question is other than "myself," the art of magick has not been understood.
- Magick is not an excuse for a life-style. The energy that you put into looking like a magician is far better spent doing the work of one. Magical growth never comes through the regard of others. It is a truism in magick that your inner accomplishments, are in most cases, inversely proportional to your outer reputation for magical accomplishment. Adepts are a quiet and unassuming group on the whole, with a few notable exceptions.
- Magick is not about gaining status or degrees. Magick is not about social presence or enhancing your reputation or self-image, except in that magical growth will eventually lead to all of these things as those around you notice the inner changes taking place.
- Magick is not about becoming famous, or notorious, or developing famous or infamous friends. Magick is about magick. Fame is about fame. Notoriety is about notoriety. Each to its purpose.
- Magick is about inner work. Great concern must be placed

upon inner work and inner change for the progress of magick to take place. Over time, attention may once again turn to the outside world. Or you may perhaps discover that the outside world isn't outside at all.

- Magick is about profound inner change that no one but yourself may ever see. We all share a tendency to desire the recognition of others when we have accomplished something. This recognition is unimportant in spiritual matters. In fact, this very type of attention can prevent or slow progress on the way.

- Magick is concerned with connection to the deeper self and connection to spirit.

- Magick is much more than a role-playing game or fantasy of the mind.

- Magick is a way of life and a state of mind, every day, every hour, every moment, in every action.

- The most basic prerequisite for successful magical study is a willingness to change.

- Magick can never do anything for you. It works through you. It is only through your own effort that magick can accomplish anything at all. To stand in your circle and call upon the gods to obtain a new job for you is akin to standing by a proposed well and calling upon the shovel to dig it for you. Call on magick for help, but pick up the shovel and dig.

- Magick involves working with existing currents, learning to call upon them, to find them within, to direct them. The laws of physics still apply and nothing is truly created or destroyed, only directed and changed. This single aphorism is more important than all those that have gone before.

2

FIRST STEPS
INTO MAGICK

The practice of magick is enhanced greatly when we develop practice routines and make observation of the cycles around us. These help the practitioner keep in touch with the currents of this and other realms. One example of such practice is our observance of the Sun's motion through the heavens each year, with formal recognition of the four solar festivals (Winter and Summer Solstice, Spring and Fall Equinox), as well as the four fire festivals (Imbolc, Beltaine, Lughnasadh, and Samhain). Another, perhaps more important practice, is the personal daily work that each magician performs to bring light, spirit, and magick into day-to-day life. Crucial to this daily work is the ceremonial observance of the rising and setting of the Sun.

FIRST MAGICAL RITE: THE SOLAR ADORATION

The spiritual Sun and the aspiration toward light play a large role in Aurum Solis philosophy and practice. In a pre-initiatory welcoming rite used at Lapis Lazuli, we attune the probationer to our goals and current. In the rite's invocation of light is this lovely borrowing from T. S. Eliot's "Choruses from The Rock:"

O Light Invisible, we praise Thee!
Too bright for mortal vision.
O Greater Light, we praise Thee for the less; The
    eastern light our spires touch at morning,
The light that slants upon our western doors at
    evening,
The twilight over stagnant pools at batflight,
Moon light and star light, owl and moth light,
Glow-worm glowlight on a grassblade.

O Light Invisible, we worship Thee!
We thank Thee for the lights that we have kindled,
The light of altar and of sanctuary;
    Small lights of those who meditate at midnight
And lights directed through the coloured panes of
    windows
And light reflected from the polished stone,
The gilded carven wood, the coloured fresco.
Our gaze is submarine, our eyes look upward
And see the light that fractures through unquiet water.
We see the light but see not whence it comes.
O Light Invisible, we glorify Thee![1]

In line with the spirit of this pre-initiation rite is the first daily routine a student of Aurum Solis magick should establish: the Solar Adoration. This ritual is performed twice each day, once in the morning and once again in the evening. If possible, the adorations should be done at sunrise and sunset while facing the rising/setting Sun, or as near to these events as your schedule allows. This adoration is best performed outdoors, as weather allows, for reasons you will come to understand in the course of your own performance of the rite.

There are several reasons for the regular performance of this adoration. An Aurum Solis paper describes it thus:

> [The] Sun is the supreme symbol and representative of spiritual power in our world, just as the physical rays of the Sun are in fact the source of light, warmth, health and energy. Giving a few moments of time at the two critical moments in the day, sunrise and sunset, to align oneself physically and mentally with this source, is thereby to stand in harmony with the currents of life and well-being on every level. Furthermore, since the visible Sun is but the "created manifestation" of the Power to which in reality the adoration is addressed, the habitual use of "solar adoration" builds up a real perception of the spiritual underlying the physical, the "Sun behind the Sun," and thus establishes the student in rapport with the spiritual world.

Further, on the significance of the moments of sunrise and sunset:

> The Sun-sphere essentially signifies the Eternal made manifest in the transient moment. Those who honor dawn and sunset, day after day, winter and summer, grow in the awareness that though these phenomena are

in a sense "always the same," yet in another sense they are never twice alike: each new day, each new evening produces wonder ever new.

The adoration used in Aurum Solis is drawn from Hindu scripture, the solar invocation found in the *Isha Upanishad*, with some modifications. The *Isha Upanishad* is perhaps the most highly regarded of this type of spiritual writing among Hindus. The etymology of the word *upanishad* suggests sitting at the feet of a great master. Perhaps these grand poetic works of India's distant past were indeed attempts to capture the teachings of ancient masters and teachers.

Of the *Isha Upanishad*, Mahatma Gandhi once said that, if all the *Upanishads* and all the other scriptures happened all of a sudden to be reduced to ashes, and if only the first verse in the *Isha Upanishad* were left in the memory of the Hindus, Hinduism would live forever.[2] The *Isha Upanishad* calls to us in brilliant poetry to look to the real and discard the unreal. As a grand work of mystical literature, the *Isha* is an invocation of the light within, the Sun at the center of our being, the true self and Higher Genius that lies at the core of our being and defines our existence. These lines of the *Isha* strike a chord of familiarity in all who aspire to the light:

> The face of the truth is hidden by your orb
> Of gold, O sun. May you remove your orb
> So that I, who adore the true, may see
> The glory of truth. O nourishing sun, Solitary traveler,
>   controller,

Source of life for all creatures, spread your light
And subdue your dazzling splendor
So that I may see your blessed Self.
Even that very Self am I![3]

Adapted and aligned to the Western mysteries and the Ogdoadic current, this deeply moving call to the hidden Sun becomes our daily invocation of the mystical Sun, and our own Higher Genius.

The Aurum Solis Solar Adoration Rite

Salutation and praise unto thee,
    O life-enkindling Sun, child of Creation's Lord!

O thou lone all-seeing Eye of the vault celestial!
Extend thy light that I may see,
but dim thy glory that I be not blinded.

Unmask thy countenance, O God of Light:
for I am a lover of Truth
and I would behold the spiritual essence concealed by
    thy golden disk!

So reveal unto my perception
thy shining and inmost nature,
even that high spirit which infuses thee
and is one with the primal flame
of mine own being.

O life-enkindling Sun,
child of Creation's Lord:
Salutation and praise unto thee!

The Solar Adoration, as I wrote earlier, is performed twice each day, once in the morning and once in the evening. It is traditional, and beneficial, if the morning adoration comes as close to sunrise as possible, with the evening adoration at the moment of sunset, but the busy day-to-day lives of most people precludes such monastic practice. It is sufficient that the morning adoration take place shortly after rising, and the evening adoration as close as conveniently possible to sunset. It is much better to perform the Solar Adoration twice daily under whatever conditions than to only perform it when conditions are perfect.

The Solar Adoration Rite

1. Stand facing the rising or setting sun, as appropriate.
2. Relax, taking several deep breaths. Let your arms relax at your sides.
3. Raise your arms to the sides, palms up, until they are approximately shoulder height.
4. Close your eyes, visualizing the rising or setting sun, as it appears before you. Contemplate the symbolic meaning of the Sun.
5. Speak the Solar Adoration out loud, with feeling and meaning. Do not hurry through this or let it become a rote recitation. Be dramatic, and let each phrase echo within you.
6. After speaking the Adoration, pause and reflect again on the spiritual principles just spoken.
7. Lower your arms to your sides and take one more cleansing breath.

3

MAGICAL ETHICS

Magick, in various forms, is found in everything from Disney's *Fantasia*, to the witches of Shakespeare and the *Wizard of Oz*. Throughout them all, a subtle theme recurs: ethics. Good witches and bad witches, white magick and black magick, helpful wizards and evil sorcerers. Magical texts discuss the "left-hand path" and "right-hand path" or contrast "Black" magick to "White" magick. The *Wizard of Oz* has both good witches (North and South) and bad witches (East and West). It is very difficult to write on the subject of magick in any context without engaging in a discussion of ethics. Some writers state and restate the so-called Threefold Law, while others spend page after page denying the necessity of magical ethics.[1]

Through religious and philosophical writing from the dawn of time to the present day, the issue of right and wrong has been almost obsessively pursued. The question of ethics has been part of the question of humanity since the first thefts and murders took place in a social context. The question has been a hot one, from Adam and Eve to the newspaper headlines of tomorrow, making and breaking entire religions and planting the seeds of war.

If you are looking to this chapter for a list of things to do and not to do with magick, you won't find much here. As we grow in our ability to affect the world around us, however, we grow in the responsibilities inherent in these powers and new abilities.

This issue is by no means limited to magick. A physician has a higher level of ethical responsibility, for example. Who could convincingly argue that the full range of pharmaceutical drugs should be available at the local market? Ethical questions of diagnosis, prognosis, prescription, and disclosure have little bearing however, until one has achieved the education and experience required to write prescriptions in the first place. The study of the Western mysteries, and the increasing ability to put them to use, carries much the same responsibility, as the consequences of a magician's actions potentially have a much wider scope than the consequences of a single prescription.

The question thus becomes, given this new ability to understanding the essential nature of the cosmos, how do we conduct ourselves? This is not a question that can be answered with a final, authoritative set of written ethics (on a tablet of stone, perhaps?). What we need to know is how ethics work. We need to develop tools with which to apply this decision-making process "on the fly" as new situations arise. It is an ancient aphorism in the philosophical study of ethics that a man is far more likely to cheat on other people's rules than his own.

As Aleister Crowley advised a student in his *Magick Without Tears:*

> But as to your own wit of judgement as to the general
> rules of your own private Code of Morals, what is "right"

and what is "wrong" for you, that will emerge only from long self-analysis such as is the chief work of the Sword in the process of your Initiation.[2]

MAGICK AND ETHICS

The etymology of the word *ethic* begins with early Greek philosophers who coined the term *ethikos* from the earlier term *ethos*, meaning "custom." Certainly, the issue of right versus wrong was discussed exhaustively before the Greeks—for example, discussions of good and evil behavior in some early Egyptian and Babylonian texts. The Greeks, however, appear to have been the first to make it a science, and a human process based on something other than divine authoritative directives.

It is important to distinguish ethics from morals. In the Western traditions, *ethic* is the bigger word, a general term denoting our feelings or thinking about right and wrong. A *moral* value, religious or otherwise, is just one of many influential factors in developing our ethics. Many in our society resist words like "ethical" and "morality," preferring other terms such as "social justice," "aesthetics," "principles" or "integrity." They all mean essentially the same thing. We each have a code of conduct within us by which we guide our own actions and judge the behavior of others. Despite current New Age ideas about enlightened nonjudgment,[3] most of us will protest when faced with those who hold a code of conduct that comes into conflict with our own most cherished rules.[4]

Ethics in magick basically boils down to a conscious ongoing analysis of our inner code of conduct and the increasing reliance on the true self for guidance in such matters. Initially, the most important task is to understand from whence our ethics come. Far beyond whatever philosophical position may appeal to the individual, from "Do no harm" to "The Golden Rule," to "Do what thou wilt," the holy indwelling genius guides us unerringly to that which fulfills our purpose in this life. That very flame of inspiration at the heart of our being is the true star, our guide in all things.

Until progress has been made on the way of return, however, this is often a dimly heard voice. We frequently talk ourselves out of our inner sense of right and wrong, usually for reasons derived from somewhat less lofty goals.[5]

If magick were a religion, we could simply state what the goddesses and gods have said is right and wrong and be done with it. This common method of defining a sense of right and wrong serves us well as children, when we need external guidance toward socialization. For adults, especially those living the magical way, it simply will not and should not suffice. External authority must give way to internal authority in the realization of the Higher Genius within, and the True Will.

THE ACTION-REACTION PRINCIPLE

> [In this case] the tourbillon [vortex of energy] will not touch the victim for whom it was destined; but the very fact of the existence of the tourbillon brought some local break in the balance of the surrounding astral forms. The astral environment must then attain a newly balanced state by the creation of a cliche of that balance (nothing perishes in Nature)...the energy he [the operator] has created will react against himself. This is known as the "return blow."[6]

All magick is subject to the action-reaction principle. In this way, magick is very much like physics: every action has a reaction. The cosmos is not judgmental about this, and the so-called Threefold Law rarely, if ever, applies.[7] As in physics, every action has an *equal* and *opposite* reaction. The entire universe is built on this principle. We see it in our lives in everything from the crack of a baseball bat, to the small waves in our bathtubs, to the ebb and flow of Earthly tides in their slow dance with the Moon.

While this principle is entirely amoral, the action-reaction principle is always present. It is often difficult, however, to foresee where in one's life it will appear. Take, for instance, the case in which you have created some vortex of energy and directed it in anger or sexual desire at another person. There are two possible outcomes from this act:

- The energy will indeed reach the person you intend, who will react to it, either becoming ill or suddenly desiring you. This reaction to your action completes the Law of Return, though other laws apply that may make the whole situation less pleasant than you initially thought.

- On the other hand, magical operations such as these are by no means as easy to direct as it may appear, and the object may take defensive action of some sort, causing your vortex of energy to "miss" its target. In this case, the energy will then seek out the next most powerful astral connection to itself, and this is your own intent and desire for the action to come about. Thus, you fall ill, or lust hopelessly after your intended target. This is what is often called a magical rebound. The history of magick is filled with tales of such events.[8]

In general terms, we have often seen that those who are hateful and angry toward others tend to become increasingly more hateful and angry themselves. Magick simply magnifies this basic principle. Likewise, it is well known among those who work to draw down the light into our world that their actions bring ever-increasing light into their own lives and the lives of those around them.

In all magick, and especially practical magick, the best guide is always to look within yourself and work to change yourself rather than other people. To accomplish something in magick, it is far easier and far less messy to change yourself than to change the people and environment around you.

When using magick to affect something outside yourself, as a general rule, remember the laws of physics: direct magical energy at others only when you are prepared for it to rebound on you. Divination can be helpful in determining the likelihood of success in a magical operation. We will cover this subject shortly.

RESPONSIBILITY

Carl Glick, in a delightful little book titled *The Secret of Serenity*, relates the following story:

> Quite gaily, as if it were of no consequence, [my friend Chao] said: Recently I lost a lot of time and money. My business partner, Hsu, whom I trusted, didn't fulfill his promises. He trimmed me out of my share of the profits and left me neatly holding the bag.
>
> Tough luck, I said.
>
> Yes, I suppose so, he answered, But I can't blame him. You see, it was really my own fault.

Your fault? I asked in astonishment. When a man is dishonest and not trustworthy?

Exactly, responded Chao. Had I proceeded as I should have—philosophically—this might not have happened.

What has philosophy got to do with another man's being dishonest? And why is it your fault, and not his?

It's really very simple, said Chao, Sort of like sitting on a hot stove....Should I sit on a hot stove and get burned, is it the fault of the stove because it was too hot? Or is it my fault because I was too cool? It's my fault entirely. I should have examined the stove first to see how hot it was. But I didn't—and so got burned. I'd be very unreasonable if I blamed the stove wouldn't I? It's that way exactly with my business partner and myself....So, under the circumstances I have no one to blame but myself. I presume it would be much easier to alibi my misfortune by blaming Hsu....But why should I add another mistake to the first I had already made?[9]

Certainly, this is not to say that, in such a case, one would not attempt to recover stolen money, or use a lawsuit to achieve recompense for the actions of another, or even to use magick to aid one's cause in that lawsuit. It is important, however, to place responsibility where it belongs, and realize that the best use of magick in such cases is the inner work that results in a growth in wisdom that can prevent such occurrences from happening in the future. To use magick as a tool of revenge against an offending party will, in the long run, cost you far more than you will ever get out of it.

Moreover, there are subtle aspects to using magick to manipulate others. Take, for instance, the example of approaching a person for a loan. There are two magical approaches available: either use magick to manipulate or influence the other person to give you the money, or use magick to make yourself into someone to whom that person would decide to loan money using their normal judgment. Describing a similar choice, Aleister Crowley wrote in *Magick Without Tears:*

> Suppose that by what is hardly fraud, but undue influence (as the lawyers say) I could persuade a dying person to leave me a couple of hundred thousand in his will. I shall use every penny of it for the Great Work; it sounds easy! Of course! Damn your integrity! Damn you! The Work is all that matters.
>
> All the same, I say NO. I should never be the same man again. I should have lost that confidence in myself which is the spine of my work. No need that the fraud should be discovered openly: it would appear in all my subsequent work, a subtle contamination.[10]

In practice, we can never actually use magick to change someone else without a corresponding change in ourselves, for better or worse.

WHITE AND BLACK MAGICK

Personally, I do not subscribe to concepts of black and white magick, left- and right-hand paths, and similar divisions of magick into two intents, one good and one evil. There is a dualism in magical action, but this is best understood as being akin to positive and negative charges of electricity, north and south poles of a magnet, the growth of spring and the death of fall, yang and yin. Yin is not bad, and yang is not good. Rather, both are necessary to the conduct of the cosmos. Moreover, the yin/yang symbol so familiar to us contains a white dot amid the black and a black dot amid the white to indicate that these principles interact intensely. There is nothing in the cosmos that is entirely yin or entirely yang.[11]

It is, nonetheless, true that acts of magick may be divided into two types without reference to color: high magick, or that which is devotional in nature or performed in a working with one's own highest goals and aspirations; and practical magick, in which rites are oriented primarily toward effects on the physical plane.

Acts of practical magick that are at the extremity of yin—having to do with destruction, reduction, and contraction—and those that are at the extremity of yang—having to do with creation, growth, and expansion—require great wisdom to understand their extraordinarily complex implications. Thus even the adept is cautioned against acts of destruction unless something better can be put in place. The true adept proceeds cautiously when introducing any grand act of new creation into the balance of the cosmos.[12]

WORKING MAGICK ON BEHALF OF OTHERS

Without the discussion above, you probably instinctively know that you should not use magick to harm or kill another person,[13] just as you should probably not harm or kill a person with any tool except in the gravest of circumstances. It is equally wrong to help or heal others through magick without their express knowledge and permission. As Dion Fortune wrote:

It may be laid down as a maxim in spiritual healing that no one has the right to apply any alterative mental treatment to another without that person's consent. Is it too much to expect that you should write to that person, stating what you propose to do, and obtain his consent before you submit him to a course of treatment? If you have any reason to suspect that such consent might not be forthcoming, is that a justification for giving the treatment without his knowledge? ...Many people have profound religious convictions, and would consider such interference blasphemous. Even if we do not agree with them, we ought to respect their opinions. ...Is there anybody who has sufficient wisdom to know the needs of another soul?[14]

As another example, imagine that your magical activities come to the attention of a serious and rather traditionally religious Christian, who begins to pray for you regularly, beaming prayerful thoughts to you that your acts are evil and must be ended. While your wards may fend off such attentions, if you become aware of this energy, do you welcome it? The intention of this person is entirely good, for he or she believes deeply that prayer will save your soul from eternal damnation. Does this, however, give that person the right to interfere with how you have chosen to live your life?

No one likes to be manipulated, and working magick for others is manipulation of a very subtle kind, unless the recipient has given permission. Even magical healing can be unwelcome, as illness serves a purpose for some.

Finally, on this matter of ethics, let me leave you with this idea from Rumi:

Make trial of yourself as to weeping and laughter, fast-
ing and prayer, solitude and company, and the rest,
which of these is more profitable to you. Whichever
state brings you straighter on the road and secures your
greater advancement, choose that task. Take counsel of
your heart, even if the counselors counsel you. The
truth is within you: compare with it the counsel of the
counselors and where it accords with that, follow that
counsel.[15]

A TAROT CARD DIVINATION

One method used by magicians to make ethical decisions
about rituals and other magical acts is to perform a tarot card divination to see what the future may hold for the effects of the magical rite. If you don't already have one, you should obtain a deck of
tarot cards, and you should accustom yourself to the tarot, as it
plays a crucial part of the Western mystery tradition. Select a deck
that is traditional in design, yet appeals to you on an emotional
level. Tarot cards tend to have personalities of their own. Just as
with people, there are some you will like and some you will not.

For at least the first six months of using the tarot, separate the
Major Arcana cards from the *Minor Arcana* cards. The major cards
are those with names and pictures such as The Magician, The Fool,
The Wheel of Fortune. The minor cards are those with suits, such
as the Three of Disks or the Princess of Wands. The minor cards are
important, but the cards of the Major Arcana have the widest influence. Begin with them.

Obtain one or more books about tarot, again relying upon your
own senses to find those that are in harmonious vibration with

your inner self. While there are many books that give card meanings and spreads, Aurum Solis uses a slightly different set of card meanings. These, and a great deal of other information about the tarot, are contained in the excellent *Magick of the Tarot,* by Denning & Phillips.

When inquiring about smaller matters, I often use a quick three-card spread that shows the basic ideas at work. I'll do a larger spread if I have questions or doubts about these three.

To perform the three-card spread, shuffle the deck of Major Arcana cards three times, while centering your thoughts on the magical act you intend. Frame these thoughts as a question. When you have finished shuffling, cut the deck and put down the cards. Quiet your mind and assume a state of open receptivity, letting the energetic Currents around you touch upon your inner senses. Then, deal three cards from the top of the deck. Place the first in the middle, the second to the left, and the third to the right. (See figure 1, page 27.)

The card in the middle represents the present, and the present currents as they pertain to your intended act. The card on the left represents the immediate past, and the currents from the past that are affecting the present. The card on the right represents the future, and completes the flow of current from the card of the past, through to the card of the present, to the future.

Examine the three cards as a unit. Look up their meanings and symbolism, but weigh these given meanings with your own "gut" feelings about what the cards are telling you. The study of tarot can occupy a lifetime by itself. The archetypal keys of these ancient cards are doors that can open up great insight into ourselves, into magick, into Qabalah, and into the very process of energy flowing into manifestation.

Figure 1. A three-card tarot spread.

When you are finished, record the session: the date, the time, the question, which cards were drawn, your interpretation of them, and anything else that drew your interest or that you sensed during the reading. Put the cards back into the deck, and finish the divination with a deep cleansing breath.

4

CALL TO THE JOURNEY

Now that we have explored the idea of magick a bit more, it's time for another important task: the evaluation of the ordinary world. To be ready for growth and change requires a serious understanding of where you are, just as a map to a destination is only of value if you know how it relates to your current position.

BUILDING FOUNDATIONS

In the study of magick, we often see students in a rush to learn practices that reach into the higher levels of existence and experience. Astral projection, Qabalistic pathworking, divination, and assumption of god forms are all popular terms often heard in groups of neophyte magicians. This interest is natural, as these terms have a certain amount of glamour attached to them, each evoking tales of magick from story, song, and film. Without an understanding of your starting place and a good solid grounding in basic techniques, however, your reach into these realms is limited. Astral projection is of relatively little use if you do not already have a good understanding of the astral world and its mechanics. Qabalistic pathworking is superficial and shallow if you do not have a solid grounding in Malkuth, the starting point on the Tree. Modern humans have a strong tendency to deny who and where they are in favor of fictions they create, and to look for quick escapes from current situations. Yet we must build anew from what we have. There is nothing that will allow us to avoid that process.

This tendency to avoid the here-and-now is a dangerous trait in a magician. It has been remarked by many magicians over the centuries that those who venture higher on the Tree than their development allows will fall back along the paths to their true level. This is true, and is seen again and again throughout history. From experiences such as these arise the tales of magick leading to insanity.

You can learn much about yourself by looking at your own world with all the objectivity you can manage. Each of us lives his or her own myth, and we use that myth to explain away uncomfortable aspects of our lives, or to project them onto others, while strengthening those parts of ourselves we like best. This view lacks the objectivity that comes with spiritual progress, but these stories are what make our day-to-day existence interesting. It is important, nonetheless, to understand that there is nothing wrong with having such personal myths. They give us a framework for understanding and allow us to work with parts of our life toward the eventual reward of integration. One benefit of the magical way is that it gives us the perspective and ability to know when we are living a myth and when we are not—to know the strength and weaknesses of each particular personal myth and to apply them as tools for negotiating our lives.

Through a gradual understanding of the self, the adept may choose the myths and masks of life, throwing him- or herself into each one the way fine actors immerse themselves in the characters they portray. The adept is free to do this, for there is never a doubt about what is myth or mask and what is real; there is never a confusion between actor and character. Thus every character and every story may be appreciated for its value to the greater self. Indeed, the adept has found the ultimate actor in his or her life—the Higher Genius.

Begin this process with an examination of specific areas of your present life, striving for fairness and objectivity to whatever degree possible. Over time, you will find objectivity easier to obtain for the reasons cited above. Useful areas of continuing self-examination include your family life, your relationship to parents and siblings, your work life and education, your attitude toward possessions, your emotional and religious life, your possesion or lack of discipline, and your ethics. There are many more. About each of these areas, ask yourself questions and record your answers or create stories illustrating some bit of personal history. Over time, ask these same questions again and note how your perception of the questions and answers changes. Remember, this analysis is not to please anyone else. It need not fit into any accepted psychological framework. In fact, it is best not to attempt to fit your thoughts into the convenient boxes of modern psychology. The goal is not to create a list of what is wrong in your life. The goal is to provide a means by which you can see how you, the actor, are moving through your daily existence. Write, draw, sing, paint, or otherwise illustrate your personal myth!

THE MAGICAL PERSONALITY

The magical personality is one of the masks discussed above—one deliberately developed by the magician. It is a self greater than your everyday self, one that is closer to light, clothed in light, striving for light. It matters not what your situation in the real world may be, for the magical self is continually in the presence of the Divine.

The magical personality is built up, layer by layer, over the life of the magician. Eventually, the magical personality ceases to be something you put on in the temple or during rituals. It becomes your everyday mask of choice, for it is the self through which your true self and True Will flow into the world.

THE CHAMBER OF ART: THE BOMOS, THE LAMP, AND THE CHAIR

The Chamber of Art is described in one Aurum Solis Order Document as follows:

> In your following of the Magical Way you will need to establish a focal point for your activity. A place in which you can craft implements, spend time in meditation, offer your devotions to the Powers of Light and perform rituals, all while being undisturbed by the round of daily activity or by family or other commitment. Ideally, a room should be set aside exclusively for this purpose; but if this is not possible, your bedroom will serve, or you may be able to arrange to have sole use of a family room—the sitting-room, say, or a study—at agreed times.

This advice is sound and the conditions described are necessary for the advanced practitioner. When starting out, however, it may not be possible for you to find a room that you can declare your own for magical use. Do not let this keep you from putting into practice any of the exercises given later in this book. If you must use a different room on different days, or do your ritual work out-doors on a hilltop, or even in the shower stall once in a while, no harm is done and you benefit no less. It is, however, important that you have a place where you can do occasional rituals in total or near-total darkness.

Eventually, you will want to establish a more-or-less permanent area for your magical work. There is a sort of atmosphere that builds up in a room when you have been doing regular rituals and worship in it. This helps to strengthen and ease the working of your subsequent rituals. If you have the ability to set aside a room for magical purposes, don't get carried away in decorating it. Leave the room as empty as is convenient and let your own practice dictate what must be there. Try to limit the decorations and other items in your Chamber of Art to only that which is necessary for your purpose. In this, as in many things, less is more.

This room or area is known as your Chamber of Art.[1] When you are working, it should contain a few required items: a Bomos, a lamp, and a chair (see figure 2, page 35).

The Bomos

The Bomos is a small altar that is placed in the center of the Chamber of Art during rituals and other work. It should be upright rather than tablelike, though even a small folding table will suffice in the beginning and when traveling. Its form recalls those altars that, in antiquity, graced the temples of Assyria and Egypt, Greece and Rome. It represents the world of matter, resting passive and receptive beneath the power of eternity. The Bomos is a highly personal tool. Use your intuition and inner senses to choose or construct one, rather than following the plans or specifications given in books on magick. Over time, you will undoubtedly obtain or construct more than one Bomos, as your appreciation of its symbolism changes. Let dreams, visions, and other contacts with the inner self be your guide.

Outdoors, the Bomos may be any convenient flat-topped rock, tree stump, fallen log, or other natural feature. In fact, when working with nature and the four elements, such naturally occurring Bomos are powerful to the purpose indeed. To the student of magick, such occurrences are anything but accidental: they are nothing less than messages from nature calling us to worship!

The Lamp

Place a single lamp on the Bomos. This symbolizes the eternal flame or godhead, that vital splendor that sustains the worlds and resides ever at the heart of creation. It should be simple, with a single flame, and it should have had no prior use. In selecting a lamp, rely on your magical, rather than your aesthetic sense. Pick a lamp that draws you to it, not one that matches the carpeting. The lamp is lit at the beginning of any magical practice or meditation, and extinguished with the activity's conclusion. Always light and extinguish the lamp with full awareness of what it represents, and with all the reverence that should be given to this symbol of the divine light.

Outdoors, a small white candle may serve as the lamp, but be sure that this candle has no other use and that you treat it with all the reverence of the lamp in your Chamber of Art, for its light represents a larger fire and flame.

The Chair

As stated in Order documents, this should be a straight-backed wooden chair, but any seat—even a folding chair—will do. The chair should be of comfortable height for a good sitting posture, and you should be able to gaze comfortably upon the surface of your altar when seated. The chair should be comfortable enough for long stretches of meditation, yet not so comfortable that you are tempted to nap rather than meditate.

Figure 2. Model Chamber of Art.

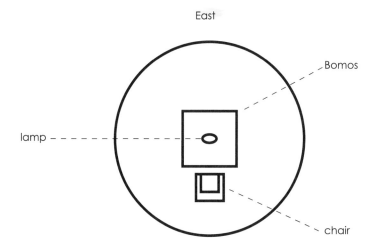

5

STUDY AND PRACTICE, YIN AND YANG

Like all journeys, the Path of Regeneration must be experienced, not read. While I would not dissuade someone from taking an academic interest in magick and going no further, a magician is more than this, much more. The transformation and rebirth of the Way of Return is a serious commitment from which, once started, one may not retreat. It requires study and practice, and integration of the Magical Way into one's day-to-day life and one's view of the world. As it is written in the Mishnah, "When one's knowledge is greater than one's deeds, the knowledge is futile."

In magick, study and practice must balance one another. Study is the quiet, contemplative, yin aspect of magick; practice is its active, yang aspect, driven by will and inspiration. Practice without study is only somewhat more useful than study without practice, and leads to a development very different from that of the magician. Both study and practice are needed to achieve the balance necessary between knowledge and wisdom, practice and experience—one of many balances found in the study of our ancient mysteries.

There were apparently three forms of teaching made use of in these [ancient Greek mystery] rites: these were λεγομενα, things said; δεικνυμενα, things shown; and δρωμενα, things performed or acted.[1]

Magick is not just something we do; it is something we are. It is not just a system of practices, but also a way of life. There is nothing in your world that will remain the same after the study and practice of magick, yet there is no task for which effort is rewarded so greatly. For the reward is wholeness, surety of purpose, and grand perspective. The reward is nothing less than true freedom, in a sense that may only be fully understood by those who have achieved it.

TIME FOR STUDY AND PRACTICE

Some years ago, during my second year of seminary, I was allotted the task of sweeping the dining room floor after each meal. I took on this task happily, but as the weeks went by, I began to grow tired of this boring, thrice-daily job. My impatience getting the better of me, I found our Prior and asked how long I would be assigned this menial task, trying to impress him with my sincere dedication to the study of theology and my desire to get on with more spiritual endeavors. "You will continue to sweep the floor for as long as you find it menial," was the gentle response. In time, with a shift of thinking rather than a shift of tasks, I came to understand what he was trying to teach me.[2]

It is difficult to estimate the time required daily or weekly for the study of magick. Individual progress varies, and, eventually, in the course of magical development, time itself is perceived differently. We each will apply ourselves as we are able, and we all move through cycles of near-total dedication to the magical life and near-total neglect of study and practice. Over time, you will almost certainly find, as most magicians do, that your life will mysteriously rearrange itself to make available the time needed.

What is most important is consistency. If possible, put aside a set amount of time each day, at the same time of day, and stick to it. Thirty minutes of combined reading, study, ritual, writing, and other activities every day will prove far more useful than the application of eight hours just one day a week. Spend a few minutes each morning and evening performing the Solar Adoration (see page 14), and begin and end your times of study, reading, and meditation with the Calyx (see page 100). Even on the busiest days, find time for the Adorations and at least one performance of the Calyx, perhaps during a break at work. Each night, before falling asleep leave yourself with suggestions for dreams and remember your dreams.[3] Wake each morning and record any dream that seems important or particularly interesting. Especially note dreams that tend to stay with you, or from which imagery or symbolism recur throughout the day.[4]

These cycles of study and practice will become more natural as you progress, and your magical work will become a constant star in what can otherwise be a bewildering world of stress and sudden change. No matter how good the day or how bad, no matter how big the lottery winnings or the demands of the tax collector—morning adoration, devotion/magick/study, evening adoration. As the ocean tides move in concert with the phases of the Moon, as the Sun rises and sets, as the stars dance in their heavenly orbits—morning adoration, devotion/magick/study, evening adoration. This basic routine is a fundamental rhythm of magick and much progress may be made on the Way of Return doing no other magical ritual or work. The priests of ancient times did little more on a daily basis, and entire modern religions were founded upon such a rhythm.

Eight times a year, the Sun moves through one of several festival days. Just as the Solar Adoration helps to accustom you to the daily cycles of the Sun, the solar and fire festivals attune you to larger cycles of time and seasonal change. Celebrate these in groups or alone, with ritual, prayer, meditation, or simply have a dinner party, a musical gathering, or a bonfire on the beach.[5]

At the Lapis Lazuli Commandery, we alternate between formal and casual celebrations of these festivals. At times, we celebrate the changes of the year in formal dramatic rites drawn from Greek and pagan traditions. Yet on the occasion of a recent Summer Solstice, we met one evening on a local beach and gathered around a bonfire. Each member of Lapis Lazuli brought an instrument—everything from drums, to harmonicas, to guitars. One person simply clicked two sticks together for rhythm. For several hours that evening, we played whatever impromptu music occurred to us, led by two drummers playing Brazilian style. We each took turns "soloing" to express in rhythm or melody our expression of this festival of light and fire. And who is to say which type of celebration accomplished more for the participants! Magick is much more than robes and tools.

How to Read

> You in the West say O God, O God! but you have no definite knowledge or methods by which you can attain to see God. It is like a man who knows there is ghee (butter) to be got out of a cow. He walks round and round

the cow and cries, O Ghee! O Ghee! Milk pervades the cow, but he cannot find it. Then when he has learned to handle the teat, and has obtained the milk, he still cannot find the ghee.[6]

Yes, you know how to read or you wouldn't have come this far. There is reading, however, and there is reading. Fiction should simply be read in whatever manner creates the greatest dramatic impact for you. Reading magical fiction can be a wonderful way to integrate magical symbolism and thinking into your life and should not engage the analytical half of your brain overmuch.

Reading magical nonfiction, however, is not simply reading to accumulate information. The Aurum Solis documents tell us that:

> Knowledge is not the same thing as memorizing. The student who has been accustomed to preparing for examinations may tend to confuse the two; but here there is no point in producing impressively memorized lists of data. The understanding is all. The difference lies in the importance accorded to the actual words of a passage. Let the student take care whenever possible to get behind the actual words on the page, to grasp the intended meanings.

I am frequently frustrated when someone tells me, for instance, that he or she has just read a text like *The Tarot* by Mouni Sadhu, or Ficino's *Book of Life*. Yet when I ask a question based on the text—"What did you think of Mouni Sadhu's attribution of the Law of Hierarchy to the Moon card when most writers would place it with the Empress?" "Have you tried to put his mathematical approach to work?" "Did you like how Ficino wrote of conflicts between a chosen profession and the Higher Genius?"—I receive a blank stare in response.

This is not a matter of a good student talking with a bad student. It is a problem of terminology. One person says, "I have read this book" and means that he or she glanced through it over a few days the way one scans the TV listings for the week, picking out interesting bits and pieces. Another person says, "I have read this book" and means that he or she has made a six month study of the text, understands the author's thinking in detail, is capable of putting the author's system to use, and may have tested out much of the theory. The problem is that the word "read" can have different meanings.

At the Lapis Lazuli Commandery, we encourage members to be clear about the extent to which they have read a particular text, using phrases such as "I skimmed the book" for the first case cited above, and "I studied the book" for the latter case.[7]

The reading and study of magical texts takes more time and effort than reading for pleasure, but it is valuable work in every way and carries great rewards. In particular, reading within a curriculum must be done with great care and attention both to the detail of the work and the meanings behind it. By this definition of "read," a book simply cannot be studied in a matter of a day or two, but will almost certainly require an extended reading over several weeks or more. College classes teach a single text over sixteen weeks, reading, analyzing, and writing on each chapter and section. In matters as important as our path to light, we should do no less.

Further, a magical curriculum is much like an academic curriculum in mathematics in several important ways. First, there are no unimportant parts. Everything counts. In fact, the parts you like least are those most likely to result in real inner growth. Second, it is expected that, after completing the mathematical curriculum, the graduate should be able to solve a problem in advanced calculus. The mathematician who slept through trigonometry because it was "boring" is not much of a mathematician at all. This is true in magick as well.

This is the point of academic testing. Students always seem to want to know what material will be on an examination, even to the point of trying to acquire the test questions themselves, when the whole point of instruction is that, if the student has truly acquired the subject matter at hand, it shouldn't matter what's on the examination. The test is only there to sort out those students who are doing the work from those who are not.

In a magical curriculum, however, you are both the teacher and the student, and you may not rely on another to direct your reading and study or test your comprehension. This is a matter of inner work, adherence to your own high standards of study and learning, and constant testing of yourself in the magical realms. No human authority will grant you a passing or failing grade, but authorities on other planes will leave no doubt in your mind as to the degree of your comprehension.

To begin, I recommend reading with a pad of paper and a pencil at your side. Read through the work and note any passages or phrases that call out to you in one way or another. As you finish each chapter, make an outline of the main points, then go over those points in your own mind. Allow your thoughts to wander freely over these ideas and images, and note any impressions. You might find that what you have just read reminds you of something else you read before; note that, and make a point of looking up that reference later. In this way, you integrate your study and reading into your world, and connect it to other ideas and images already in your consciousness. Spend a little time weighing new ideas, and try out those that appeal to you and seem to be within your skills.

Now, go back and read the chapter or section word for word, extending this process of reading and reflection to the work in greater and greater detail. In time, you will have a firm grasp of every idea in the text, and you will have integrated into yourself many of the ideas that ring true in some way. The goal is not to be able to sit with another person and quote passages to one another, but rather to squeeze all the personal growth you can from the text.

Don't worry, at this point, that you do not possess every great book of magick currently in print. Simply to read dozens of books on magick is like having a drawer full of keys, some of which you recognize, some of which you do not, yet never opening the doors they unlock. Those who have studied five or six books of magick deeply, and have opened themselves to the corresponding inner changes that always accompany such study, will accomplish a great deal more in their lives than those who have skimmed 100 books of magical texts.[8]

Many more people study magick than practice it. Fewer still live the magical life. To be in the latter group requires paying less attention to what you read and more to how you read. Quality, not quantity, is the theme of the artisans at the Lapis Lazuli Commandery.

Let me finish this section by returning, once again, to writings from the papers of our order:

> Let the student also be watchful at all times for relation-
> ships perceived between her reading and her experience,

particularly her experience in the practice of Art Magick. All such discoveries, whether of resemblance or of dissimilarity, are of value. Let her not, certainly, seek out relationships where they do not and should not exist: both her magical sense and her common sense should be trained to safeguard her against that. This being understood, however, it is true to say that the study and practice both, undertaken and faithfully pursued, will benefit any student—even the utmost beginner— immeasurably more than either study or practice alone.

THE MAGICAL DIARY

Entire books and discourses have been written concerning the magical diary. Each of us is a unique laboratory. Because of this, magick will not work in exactly the same way in any two incarnate lives. The magical diary gives us both data and the perspective of time, and allows us to discover how magick works in our lives and what in our lives impacts our practice of the magical way. The diary is critically important to the process of magical development, for hindsight is never 20–20, but is rather colored by emotional responses to events. Our perceptions fade and alter over time. In a practical sense, your diary becomes your book of spells, not unlike such as those made by the famous magicians of history. Recording which rites work for you and which do not is a sure guide to developing rites that work every time. Moreover, your diary serves as a library of experimentation. If once, ten years before, you worked out a particularly useful rite of material gain, you may now, ten years later, re-create that rite as needed. The Order tells us that the simplest exercises have their place therein: record at what time they are performed, whether any part be omitted and for what reason, whether in your opinion your work has been well done or not. This record will assist you when from time to time you reconsider your program. It will also put you in excellent practice for when you have to record actual magical operations in your diary, for these must, unconditionally, be set down rapidly, honestly and in detail, immediately after their completion.

At the Lapis Lazuli Commandery, we ask our new members to establish three journals. This sounds more complicated than keeping one magical diary, but it actually simplifies the process considerably.[9]

The Dream Journal

First, before all else, establish a dream journal. This is a diary used for nothing else, kept by your bed with a pen or pencil. Each time you wake, either during the night or in the morning, immediately write down or draw as many and as much of your dreams as you can remember. Note any symbols that stand out to you and any personalities, either known or unknown to you. Especially note anything that corresponds to your magical activities, and try to capture as accurately as possible any dream in which a voice from the sky or writing upon a wall occurs. As you progress, two things will happen:

- You will begin to remember your dreams more accurately

and more of them. As your mind becomes accustomed to the idea that you wish to remember dreams, it will comply, and the richness and detail of the dream world will not fade as quickly in the morning light.

- You will begin to gain keys toward understanding your own inner processes. This is why so many systems of applied psychology and psychological counseling rely upon the noting and interpretation of dreams. Do not, at first, put a great deal of effort into interpreting your dreams, and be ready to accept that your first interpretations may be wrong or incomplete. Over time, many dreams will reveal themselves in greater detail and their symbolism will acquire meaning.

Dreaming is a potent vehicle of communication between your unconscious and conscious mind. The ability to monitor this communication will be of extraordinary value to you in your progress on the magical way.

The Magical Journal

Next, acquire and establish a magical journal, used for recording rites, creating new rites, tracking dates of initiations and impressions thereof, etc. This journal should be a letter-sized, three-ring notebook where you keep, not only your own rites and data, but also other magical or Order documents you may acquire over time. Keep your magical journal in your personal Chamber of Art or wherever your magical tools are stored.

This is the journal that most closely matches the great spellbooks of old, where the experiments of magick were recorded and evaluated. To enhance this impression, several Lapis Lazuli members keep their journals in three-ring binders with leather covers, often cut or branded with magical symbols.[10]

The Artisan Journal

At the Lapis Lazuli Commandery, we call our members artisans—the dreamers, shapers, singers, and makers of our magical art. The artisan journal is dedicated to this most artistic and creative side of the magician. It is a small notebook or sketchbook, usually carried on your person (when possible), in your purse or backpack, or in your car. In these small books, our artisans keep records of correspondences as they occur to them in the course of the day, ideas or images that occur during reading or on viewing theatrical presentations, unexpected visual/auditory perceptions of other realms, astrological data of note, drawings, musical scores, and on and on. As your magical diary captures your experiments with magick, your artisan journal captures your experiments with life. I strongly encourage you to begin a journal like this for yourself.

Each of these three journals represents one of the major areas of magical work: the dream journal for the astral world, the magical diary for the world of intellect and mind, and the artisan journal for the light of inspiration that drives and guides us all.

THE MAGICK RING

Rings and magick have been connected for centuries. Every great wizard of story and myth has a magick ring. Solomon himself was reputed to have designed and used rings for specific magical purposes. Our symbol of marriage is the ring and Catholic clergy wear rings declaring their station. Magicians have long claimed to create or own great rings of power. These stories led to the creation of epic tales such as J. R. R. Tolkien's *Lord of the Rings* trilogy.

In many ways, the ring is the magician's most powerful tool. It symbolizes the circle within which we stand while working rites. It is even more than this potent symbol, as the ring is a garment that, with time and the development of the magical personality, comes to symbolize the entire magical personality in one all-encompassing symbol. At any place and time, and under any circumstance, your magical personality may be brought forth merely by placing the ring on your finger.[11] Order documents enjoin us to:

> Select a ring—and it must be a new item having no past associations of use—to be your Magical Ring. It may be a plain gold or silver band, like a wedding ring, or it may be adorned with a single precious or semi-precious stone. A birthstone would be appropriate here, but another may be chosen from personal preference or motive: onyx or lapis as symbol of eternity, for instance; ruby or any red stone for divine energy; sapphire or a blue stone for spiritual abundance; emerald or any green stone for vitality, hope and inspiration.

Accustom yourself to wearing your magical ring whenever you do any sort of magical work, meditation, or devotional prayers. As one Aurum Solis document tells us, when you place the magical ring upon your finger, *know* that you are, in reality, a "person of power," that your being is attuned to cosmic forces of light and life, and that you are capable of realizing and utilizing every faculty and power that is your spiritual birthright as a child of the cosmos.

Most of the members of Lapis Lazuli carry their rings with them at all times. Many have made small pouches for them that can be carried in a pocket or bag. Having this most important of magical tools on your person keeps it available for spontaneous nature rites, the Solar Adoration, or simply a meditative time in the course of the day when you wish to don your magical personality. To wear the ring is to don your magical personality. This can be a welcome relief from the limitations and failings we believe ourselves to have. Wearers of the ring gain the perspective of re-viewing the world around them—perspective of the stars.

> Education of the psyche by means of the magical personality contains much which can validly be likened to that relaxation, that casting off of nervous tension, which makes for a truer aim in sports; that emancipation from the compulsion to succeed which is an emancipation also from the specter of failure.[12]

6

MEDITATION

Earlier, I wrote of magick as part focus and part inspiration. Meditation is one of the most powerful tools available to us for the development of focus. Yet, for the considerable peace of mind and mental focus that meditation can bring, it is a remarkably simple thing to do. In fact, we carry out the method of meditation at least once in a while, entirely by accident, without even knowing this is what we have done. The purpose of this section of study is to bring about this state deliberately, with focus, and in a way that will benefit your magical work, always heeding Ficino's excellent advice from his *Book of Life:* "While you are working with your soul, keep the body quiet. Fatigue of the body is bad, fatigue of the soul is worse, but worst of all is fatigue of both, with opposite motions distracting a man and destroying his life. Let meditation walk no further than pleasure and even a little behind.[1]

At the end of this chapter, I've given a simple meditation approach that many students at Lapis Lazuli have used with success. It is a good starting place, and the following material may be used later to help point directions for further development if you so choose. You should read through this entire section, however, before beginning a meditation practice. If you already have a meditation practice that you use regularly, by all means continue to use it, but read through this section to find clues about how to turn your meditative practices toward the greater work.

When I teach meditation classes, I often divide meditation into three areas: breath, focus, and chanting.

BREATH

> The infant draws in a long, deep breath, retains it for a moment to extract from it its life-giving properties, and then exhales it in a long wail, and lo! its life upon earth has begun. The old man gives a faint gasp, ceases to breathe, and life is over. From the first faint breath of the infant to the last gasp of the dying man, it is one long story of continued breathing. Life is but a series of breaths.[2]

Stop for a moment and pay attention to your body. What is it doing? Among the many things that may be happening to your body at this moment, the one that dominates and guides the others is the breath. Hold your breath for a few moments, then breathe deeply. Feel how your heart rhythm changes with your breath. Over time, if you work with your breathing systematically, you will find that it is your breath that regulates and inspires virtually every system in your body. In fact, the word "inspiration" means breath.

One important tool of any meditation or magical system is the development of the basic autonomic rhythm of the body. We all breathe, every minute of every day, waking or asleep, conscious or unconscious, we breathe. The simple experiment given above demonstrates the effect of breathing on the heart rate, but only hints at what may be accomplished by consciously using breath as a tool. This potential was appreciated in ancient Greece, where Galen, whose work is thought to be the culmination of work begun 600 years earlier by Hippocrates and the Pneumatist school (followers of Erasistratus), taught the principle of *pnuema zotikon* or *spiritus vitalis*—a vital spirit contained within the breath that gives life and movement to all things. The Pneumatists and other vitalists developed entire schools of medical practice around this concept, teaching the rudiments of what may be found even today in our Art Magick.

While the breath was appreciated in the West by Greek philosophers, Qabalists, early Christians, Moslems and others, two great systems from the East developed this idea to its ultimate form. These great and ancient systems arose from India and China, and may well have influenced later Western ideas on this subject.

In India, the concept of conscious breathing was developed to a high degree as one of the tools in the discipline known as *pranayama*. Pranayama is the control of prana, one of the two basic units of the universe. In Indian thought, akasha is the substance of the universe, and prana is the energy behind it, a moving, binding power of manifestation.

> Prana is in the atmospheric air, but is it also elsewhere, and it penetrates where the air cannot reach....The Hebrew writer of the book of Genesis knew the difference between atmospheric air and the mysterious and potent principle contained within it. He speaks of

neshemet ruach chayim, which, translated, means the breath of the spirit of life.[3]

Pranayama is the art and science of using meditation, breathing, and other exercises to control and direct this manifesting energy. The first step in this task is control of the breath, as Swami Vivekananda wrote:

> We have seen that the first step, according to the Yogis, is to control the motion of the lungs. What we want to do is to feel the finer motions that are going on in the body. Our minds have become externalised, and have lost sight of the fine motions inside. If we can begin to feel them, we can begin to control them.[4]

The Indian concepts of prana and pranayama are so similar to some of the basic ideas of Western magick that many great magicians of history have studied Indian Hindu and Buddhist beliefs and practices. Authors like Aleister Crowley incorporated a great deal of yoga into their magical writings.

In ancient China, Taoists developed *Qi Gong* as a method of using the breath. This vast system of techniques and applications have been a core part of religion, martial arts, and medicine in China for over 3000 years. To the early Chinese philosophers, the universe was divided into two opposite and complementary elements, yin and yang. These polarities are best understood when expressed as a series of pairs, as shown in Table 1 (see page 55).

The original Chinese characters for yin and yang meant simply "shady side of a hill" and "sunny side of a hill," respectively. Yet neither yin nor yang may be considered static ideas: each is con-

Table 1. Yin and Yang.

YIN	YANG
Cold	Hot
Dark	Light
Negative	Positive
Female	Male
Moon	Sun
Earth	Heaven
Restful	Active
Substance	Energy
Receptive	Creative

stantly and dynamically transforming into the other. The creative force of the universe, Tao, gives rise to this dynamic tension between yin and yang. From this transformation flows the life force *Qi*. Qi, like the Tao, and yin and yang, is a difficult concept to translate into English, as we have no single word that means the same thing. Energy is one common translation, but Qi is also a quality and a function.

To quote one of my favorite writers, Claude Larre, on the difficulty of rendering translations from Chinese:

> The problem is that thousands and thousands of Chinese characters and expressions are not grounded in our minds as they are in the Chinese mind. Notwithstanding the differences of appreciation the Chinese may have from one text to another, from one author to another, or from one main text to a commentator, they all belong to the same family of minds...[The] differences of views expressed in Western textbooks of Chinese medicine are just unreconcilable contradictions, if not pure nonsense. They stem from the imagination of people of different origins not sharing the same approach to life. If it is not necessary to know what Qi is, it is at least necessary to be conscious of one's own life.

> Whenever we find [a person], whether a student,
> practitioner or teacher, who knows through bodily con-
> sciousness, that he or she is a permanent product of the
> universe, and has the feeling of something on the move,
> he needs a word for expressing this, and the word is Qi.[5]

I've always been struck by the similarities between Chinese
Taoist cosmology and certain core philosophies of Qabalah. For
example, ancient Qabalists hold that the four-letter name of
God—the Hebrew letters Yod, He, Vau, and He—may be examined
in manifestation, describing the fundamental construct of the
manifest universe. Yod represents the active principle; He represents the passive principle; Vau represents the balance of opposites; and the final He represents the resulting manifestation. In
Chinese Taoist terms, this might be correlated as Yod = Yang, He =
Yin, Vau = Tao and He = Qi.

Qi gong is a system of breathwork and patterned movements
designed to harness and eventually control Qi. In Qi Gong exercises, the practitioner learns to combine specific methods for filling the lungs, precise nose-mouth balances of breathing, counted
rhythms and patterns of inhalation and exhalation, visualization
techniques, and physical movements to harness and become one
with the flow of Qi. These techniques are then applied to martial
arts and traditional medicine, as a form of exercise for the infirm
and elderly, in Taoist sexual practices, and as a meditation discipline in the Taoist traditions, to name only a few examples.

In many ways, pranayama and Qi Gong are much like the more
practical aspects of magick. The larger systems that contain them,
yoga and Taoism respectively, give practitioners access to the
philosophies and tools for spiritual aspirations and work similar

to those of Western magicians. They are parallel systems of psychology, spirituality, and metaphysics. These Eastern systems are highly effective and of vast depth; their advanced practitioners achieve a level of skill comparable to what we expect in our great Western adepts.

Yet the difficulties of working in a system conceived in a language, culture, and philosophy so different from our own cannot be overestimated. In over twenty years of study and practice of Chinese martial arts, medicine, language, and philosophy, I still find many difficulties and barriers between myself and the deeper mysteries of these great traditions.

The breathwork of ceremonial magick is a study and practice similar to yoga's pranayama and Taoism's Qi Gong, but it is presented in a framework that suits the Western mind. The images and symbols of our traditions call out to parts of us buried deep within and echo back over time, connecting us with our ancestors, incarnations, and origins. In this exploration of the traditions and practices of magick, however, we draw on the knowledge of our Eastern companions.

The Rhythmic Breath

In the Aurum Solis tradition, this basic tool of magick is called the rhythmic breath. The basic technique has been used by many Western mystery traditions and finds parallels in Japanese, Chinese, and Indian practices. The cycles of the rhythmic breath are also used in some spiritual healing traditions, leading them sometimes to be called the healing breath.

The patterns of the rhythmic breath are linked to your own heart rate. Listen to your own heart, feel the beats within your chest and tune your focus to this essential, autonomic rhythm of the flow of your body's blood and fluids. With each beat of your heart, blood is impelled down the arteries, carrying life-giving oxygen and other needed gases and nutrients to your organs and extremeties. Each beat of your heart moves exhausted blood from your body into the lungs, where it is again energized and driven back into the heart, the circle complete. Listen to this ebb and flow of inner tides, not unlike the waves of an ocean shore. Listen for a few minutes, if needed, until your heart rhythm steadies. At first, you may find that it fluctuates with your attention, but in time, it will settle.

Begin now to count your heartbeats, while paying attention to your breathing. Empty your lungs fully and breathe air into them for a count of six heartbeats. Hold this breath within you for a count of three heartbeats, then slowly release it for six more heartbeats. Upon emptying your lungs, hold them empty for three heartbeats, then begin the cycle again. The critical point in this cycle is the three heartbeats during which the lungs are empty.

If, for reasons of health or environment, it is distressing or not possible for you to hold your lungs empty for three heartbeats, then reduce the counts from 6–3–6–3 to 4–2–4–2, holding your breath for just two heartbeats at the end of the inhalation and exhalation.

This pattern of breathing alone is a powerful form of meditative practice, and is of great assistance in the performance of magical ritual and visualization. At first, merely keeping count and breathing as instructed will fully occupy your mind. Over time, however, this will become second nature to you—an easy, relaxed rhythm into which you can fall as needed, without conscious counting, even without conscious thought. Eventually, merely establishing the rhythmic breath will trigger the focus and trance states needed for serious magical practice.

Posture

While you practice establishing the rhythmic breath, practice also the three basic postures of the Aurum Solis tradition: the God-form posture, the Wand posture, and the Earth posture.

The God-form posture is a sitting posture of Egyptian origin (see figure 3). Its most essential component is that your thighs be horizontal, while your lower leg is vertical and your feet are squarely upon the floor. Your back should be held straight, your feet and knees placed side by side. Your upper arms should be loosely at your sides, hands open and palms downward on your thighs. Look straight ahead. Several Egyptian gods are shown sitting in this posture.

Figure 3. God-form posture.

In the Wand posture you stand (see figure 4). This is the posture most often used in the Aurum Solis system. Hold your head erect, your shoulders back and straight, though not stiffly so. Your arms should hang straight at your sides, slightly bent at the elbows. Place your feet side by side, parallel and pointing straight ahead. Stand straight, but relaxed. Do not slouch, but stand tall,

Figure 4. Wand posture.

for you are in the presence of the divine and your own divine self.

In the Earth posture, you stretch your body out upon the ground, flat upon your back. Your legs and arms should be straight and relaxed. Comfort is important in this posture, as it is often used for meditation and astral work, thus loose, comfortable clothing or nudity is recommended. The Lapis Lazuli robe is ample and loose enough for all three of these classic postures.

FOCUS: MENTAL DISCIPLINE

The single most important tool of magick is focus. Every other technique and practice of the Western mysteries depends upon this skill. We have all had profound moments of focus in our lives—perhaps when pursuing a much-loved hobby, or performing or listening to a favorite piece of music, or completely losing ourselves in the joy of work or the challenge of the moment. At these times, your thoughts are focused on one task. The rest of your world is screened out or diminished, time stretches or shrinks, bodily discomforts go unnoticed, temperature changes around you and in your body do not register. When you awaken from these trance-like times of focus, your body may have grown cold or hot, the time may be much later or earlier than you thought it would be, your muscles may ache and you may find that someone has been standing beside you, speaking with ever greater frustration, for the last ten minutes.

Such times demonstrate the very sort of focus that underlies magick. The work of new students is to develop their minds toward achieving these states at will and on a willed subject or visualization. As this ability is accomplished, then developed, great power lies within it. Swami Vivekananda, when writing on the subject of meditation states:

> When the mind has been trained to remain fixed on a certain internal or external location, there comes to it the power of flowing in an unbroken current, as it were, toward that point....if the mind can first concentrate upon an object, and then is able to continue in that concentration for a length of time, and then, by continued concentration, to dwell only on the internal part of the perception of which the object was the effect, everything comes under the control of such a mind.[6]

Read that last sentence again. When a mind is concentrated and focused, turned to the subtle aspects underlying our apparent reality, everything comes under its control. Many authors from the great Eastern traditions have written similar ideas about the incredible powers of concentration, focus, and meditation, as have Western magical authors such as Dion Fortune and Aleister Crowley.

In modern quantum physics, there is a theory postulating that, at the subatomic level, merely observing a system changes it, thereby biasing all such observations. That is to say that we will, perhaps, never see an atom as it independently exists, for our attention upon it changes it. While this theory may seem obscure outside the laboratory, think about it: Our attention changes our world on an atomic and a subatomic level. If this basic connection between our thoughts and our world were practiced, focused, and directed, such a mind might well have influence over the very fabric of creation.

The Western mysteries have long had traditions of meditation and contemplation, but meditation as we know it in the West today came to us quite recently, in the late 19th and early 20th centuries, from the great yogic traditions of India. Yogic meditation placed an indelible stamp upon the Western magical traditions, as magicians from Europe and America raced to newly translated books and in-person study with yogis and swamis. Toward the middle of the 20th century, meditation came to the attention of the public with such techniques as Transcendental Meditation and the Self-Realization Fellowship's kriya yoga methods that were introduced in America and Europe.

There was good reason for this intense interest in Indian meditation methods. While many traditions, East and West, taught meditation and contemplation, the yogis made a science of mental discipline and described it in a step-by-step manner that effectively demystified the cryptic teachings of other traditions.

The West, however, possessed its own great traditions of meditation and contemplation. These were chiefly developed in the monastic movements of the Western churches. In monasteries both ancient and modern, monks and nuns are taught methods of controlling and quieting the mind in preparation for prayer or visualization exercises. Such stillness of mind and control of thought is necessary to complete required monastic contemplations, such as those prescribed by St. Ignatious Loyola and St. John of the Cross.

The Eastern Christian churches developed meditative techniques and traditions as well. The use of icons in the Eastern churches as contemplative points of focus, as windows into the spiritual world, is a powerful technique from which we will borrow later for our tarot meditations.

In modern times, scientists and religious thinkers have examined meditation, bringing high technology to bear on making meditation more efficient. John Mumford, Jose Silva, Master Charles, Edwin Steinbrecher, Robert Monroe, and others have developed highly effective systems of meditation and contemplation combining visualization, posture and sound. Of these, Jose Silva's Silva Mind Control has much to recommend it to beginning students of magick. It teaches an effective tool that may easily be applied to magical work. Steinbrecher's system is recommended to the advanced beginner or intermediate student as one more oriented toward magick.

CHANTING: THE POWER OF VOICE

Some years ago, I awoke early one morning while on retreat at a Zen Buddhist monastery. The dawn air was cool as I stepped out of

Figure 5. OM in lotus.

my small, sparsely furnished room and passed through a doorway onto a covered stone walkway overlooking the main yard and gardens of the monastery. The scent of baking bread wafted toward me from the kitchens and the small sounds of breakfast preparations were the only disturbance to the quiet of the scene. Then, from a building across the gardens, I heard a single male voice sing and hold a steady bass note: "OM." After two cycles of this, a second voice, a tenor, joined in the chant. After another two cycles, a third, higher, voice joined the sound, the three voices forming a perfect major chord of "OM." Other voices joined in, one clear voice sang the syllable as a melody, dancing over the three chord notes. As the voices gained strength and beauty, the very stones beneath my feet felt as if they were responding to this vibration of "OM."

I was transported in my mind to cool, misty mountains and dry, dusty yards and streets around the world where people sat or stood and chanted or sang this same syllable—"OM." The very structure of the universe was almost visible in the vibrations of this mighty sound, as if the fabric of reality were being shaken and thereby revealing itself. The very echoes of creation surrounded me, washed over me, and flowed through me. When, after a time, the voices stopped, it seemed as if the very stars had gone out and I found tears on my face.

A few years later, I spent a week at a Benedictine monastery in Southern California, a quiet, orderly facility amid sagebrush and dusty brown hills. Throughout the day, the quiet of the studious monastic life was punctuated with the sung prayers and assemblies of the Benedictine tradition. Gregorian chants greet the dawn each morning and continue throughout the day at intervals, until the monks sing the end of their day as they sang its beginning. At first, I merely listened to these assemblies from my small cottage in the hermitage.

On the third day, I joined the monks for one full day in each of their sung prayers. By the end of the work day, at Compline, the beautiful sung prayers became vibrations that opened doors to the past. Immersed in the vibrations of these chants, I could see and feel the air of ancient churches throughout Europe and the Middle East. In each chant, I could hear the echo of 2000 years and the countless monks who had sung these same chants before. Each ancient Gregorian chant, a direct link to a time when early Christians sang their prayers, is a key to those times and connects us with the people who have sung them. I still feel as if I touched something powerful and ancient that evening.

The sound of the human voice is magical and powerful. In ancient times, nearly all prayers were sung. Early Hebrews sang their sacred scriptures. We have numerous examples of Babylonian and Egyptian religious song and chant. The Greeks and Romans sang to their gods and goddesses. Native Americans chant their prayers in dances to the gods. The Indians chant "OM." Martial arts practitioners experience the power of the spoken voice as they learn to use the yell as one of their weapons. Pagans and Wiccans engage in rhythmic, rhyming chants and songs for their celebrations of the Earth, their gods, and their goddesses.

Throughout history, the aspirations of the human heart have been expressed in song and chant more often than any other medium. Chant is integral to the human experience, and one of the most universal forms of expression, occurring in virtually every culture on Earth. In the traditions that are interwoven with the Western mystery traditions, chant has been a consistent and important tool.

There are many words, phrases, songs, and prayers appropriate for chanting. As we progress, I'll explore this further as opportunities arise in which chant may be used in your Aurum Solis work. We will revisit the principles of chant in a later ritual, the Setting of the Wards.

Below, I describe a simple meditation practice that many Lapis Lazuli students have used. Later, you will learn to modify this practice to achieve specific ends, and you will also find that the basic techniques here factor prominently in some Order rituals, such as the Rousing of the Citadels.

A Simple Meditation Practice

For this practice, you will need a quiet room or outdoor location where you will not be disturbed, something comfortable on which to sit, a bell or other bell-like object giving a pleasant, round, lasting tone, and something with which to strike the bell. Tibetan singing bowls have their place later in the program, but require too much conscious attention for this exercise. You should either dress comfortably, or perform this meditation nude or in a robe, perhaps in the morning before you dress.

Allot a specific amount of time for this practice, perhaps ten or fifteen minutes at first, and work on it daily. Do not expect to get through the entire meditation without stopping the first few times. The practice given is of great value to your magical training and should be developed slowly, and deliberately. The practice is given in three stages.

Breathing: Establish the Rhythmic Breath

Sit comfortably, either in a chair or on a pillow. Consciously relax your body, and take a few easy cleansing breaths. Begin, as described earlier, to count your heartbeats. When you are ready, establish the rhythmic breath.

Focus on a Sound: The Bell

Maintaining the rhythmic breath, pick up the bell and hold it before you, holding the striker in the other hand. Close your eyes.

Visualize yourself sitting on a grassy slope, on the side of a fragrant and beautiful mountain. At the top of the mountain is a stone castle, but you can't really see much of it from where you sit. The air is clear and fresh, and the Sun is shining down on you, pleasantly warming your body. As you build this place in your thoughts, make it as real as you can by systematically filling in the sights, sounds, colors, smells, insects, birds, animals, trees, and other details, seeing the place as you wish it to be.

When you feel as if some part of you is actually in this place, relax and gently strike the bell. Feel the vibrations of the sound transfer to your body and enter your visualization, as if a large and ancient bell had rung from somewhere within the castle above. Make sure you can clearly hear the bell within your visualization.

Strike the bell again, gently. Again, integrate the sound into your visualization. After two or three times, you will find that you can ring the bell in your visualization without needing to ring the physical bell in your hand. When you can do that, go on to the next step.

Chant: OM

As you sound the bell in your visualization and feel the echoes of it vibrating through the scene, begin chanting your exhalations with the syllable "OM." Breathe in for a count of six, hold for a count of three, breath out "OM" for a count of six, hold for a count of three. Match the musical note and cycle of the bell in your visualization with your chant, until the bell and your chant are sounding together and reverberating across the landscape.

Continue this chant for just a few minutes at first, or until the end of your set meditation practice time. Do not expect anything in particular to happen at this point, just work to fill out the visualized scene and sounds. When you are finished, stop the chant, let the visualization fade from your thoughts, and return your breathing to a relaxed, normal cycle.

You have now completed a meditation of mixed Western and Eastern traditions, bringing together several of the most important tools of magic: breath, focus, visualization, and chant. Meditations such as these will develop your astral senses, which are crucial to effective magical work.

7

ARCHETYPES: THE TOOLS OF MAGICK

The celebrated psychiatrist, C. G. Jung, and mythologist Joseph Campbell may well have been the two most influential authors of the 20th century. Certainly Jung's work on depth psychology, archetypes, and the meaning of human symbols has changed the face of modern psychology and our understanding of the human mind. Further, Jung's ideas have influenced almost every aspect of human existence, from the interpretation of dreams, to the critical analysis of art, to the understanding of the interactions between religious belief and human experience.

From the design of stained-glass windows in modern churches, to modern interpretations of the tarot, to the development of entire fields of artistic endeavor, we can scarcely turn about in this culture without seeing something of Jung's legacy. His work on alchemy as a model for human integration and development is critically important to the understanding of the process of magick, and his two crowning works in this field, *Psychology and Alchemy* and *Mysterium Coniunxionis*, are highly recommended reading for anyone pursuing magick.

When Joseph Campbell wrote *Hero With a Thousand Faces*,[1] he applied similar ideas and processes to the myths and stories that humans have told one another throughout history, over campfires and by bedsides, and as part of organized religions and mystery traditions. Through an analysis of these ancient tales, Campbell began to note a literary parallel to what Jung was postulating for the human mind: there were recurring energies, forms, characters, and objects in myths and stories across all ages and cultures. These symbols, or archetypes, trigger deep responses in us when we are exposed to them. They strike a mysterious sense of familiarity, or provide a framework through which to understand our present lives. Through them, we may trigger religious experiences, or bring forth unknown skills and talents from deep within us.

Certainly, the idea of symbols and archetypes was appreciated and used by other writers and other cultures long before Campbell's work, but he systematized the analysis of myth and story, and presented this system in a series of books accessible to the average person, as well as the scholar. The conclusions that most anthropologists come to sooner or later in their careers, Campbell turned into an analytical form.

What are archetypes? When we group like symbols together from various sources and begin to see that they all derive from a common image or symbol, we have uncovered what is known as an archetype. Archetypal water, for example, is the root image of countless water images in our languages, cultures, and dreams— wells, rivers, seas, rain, tears, ondines, etc. Each of these images has its own meaning, but there is a root meaning they all have in common. At that root we have certain attributes that all images created from the archetype will also have.

Access to these ideas from writers and researchers such as Jung and Campbell give us, as magicians, some powerful tools with which to approach our study of the magical way. There are three areas in which archetypes play a vital role in magick:

- Archetypes play a vital role in understanding the descent through the four worlds described later in chapter 11;
- In magick, we use archetypes and symbols as tools, deliberately and precisely applying them as keys to unlock and open deep aspects of our true selves;
- Our own progress in the magical way is the path of the Solar Hero: an archetypal story of regeneration and rebirth that lies at the heart of the Aurum Solis initiatory process.

Thus, it will serve us well, at this stage, to examine some of these tools so that we can begin to apply them to our understanding of the ritual and drama of magick.

JUNG'S CONCEPT OF ARCHETYPES

Jung postulated that we have preconscious potentials within us that are expressed following certain set forms or patterns. Moreover, he found these archetypal patterns and images widely dispersed across many cultures and recurring throughout human history. To explain this deep commonality among disparate peoples, he postulated a concept known as the universal unconscious, suggesting that all humans share, at a deep level, a single unconscious mind that holds these root patterns.[2] It is the universal unconcious, he suggested, that connects us.

While the concept of the universal unconscious may be debated among psychologists and theologians, it is true that, when we examine our own personal history and images and compare them to those of another person in a different culture or time period, we find that our inner lives are not as unique as we first thought. There are certain common threads in human existence. Jung's concepts of archetypes and the universal unconscious are useful tools with which to examine these threads.

The Shadow

The most accessible of Jung's personal archetypes is the Shadow, as it arises from the unconscious and mysterious within us. It is easy to access because that which we avoid, hold down, or only dimly perceive creates the images in our lives that demand the most attention. In many ways, this archetype accounts for much of the fascination we have for horror stories, ghost tales, or dark science fiction.

In older literature and myth, the Shadow appears as a dark and frightening place, such as the woods in which Hanzel and Gretel were lured and trapped. Thieves live in the woods, and evil dragons live in dark and mysterious caves. In the movie *Return of the Jedi*, Luke Skywalker is led by Yoda to face the image of his greatest fear in a dark cave. In religious writing, especially that of the Middle East, the "wilderness" plays a primary role as a mysterious place where individuals go to fast, to pray, and, sometimes, to meet a god.

It is important to emphasize here that the Shadow is not evil or bad. The evil dragon hides in the dark cave, but the cave is not evil. Hanzel and Gretel are led into the dark forest, but the forest is not evil. It is merely a place of mysterious events and figures, the dark and scary place within that contains the things we think we fear.

Often, however, analysis in the light of day shows that the cave, forest, or bedroom closet in a child's room does not contain the monsters once feared.

The Shadow also comprises our fear of our own inadequacies, failures, and inferiority. These are sides of ourselves we are often uncomfortable facing. We are most comfortable projecting our fear of the Shadow onto others, or into literature and drama. The power of the Shadow archetype appears in the dark heroes of our stories and films, such as Batman, but also in figures such as Clark Kent, the inferior, inadequate, softer side of Superman.

The Anima and Animus

These archetypes refer to basic gender ideas that are resident in all of us. All men contain within them the Anima, or female soul; all women have within them the Animus, or male soul. The three-fold aspect of female and male—child, adult, and aged—are all present within these archetypes and they appear in our personalities in many ways. A man may draw on the Anima to contact his ability to nurture, care, and heal. A woman may draw on her Animus to contact her anger, aggressiveness, or ability to fight or stick up for herself. The Animus, for a woman, is an unconscious bundle of positive and negative images of masculinity that she experiences in dreams and fantasy. The Anima is the corresponding part of the male unconscious.

In myth and story, the Animus appears most often as a strong, warrior woman—the Amazons, or modern-day Xena, Warrior Princess, or Wonderwoman. As with the Shadow, however, we often project that with which we are not comfortable. The Animus will thus also appear as a woman who is overly dependent on a father figure or other powerful male for her power or status. This archetype also appears as gods of power and gods of war.

The Anima appears most often in the projected form as a man with a strong female presence driving or guiding him. Thus we have the goddess Athena helping and directing Odysseus in his battles and voyages, or the beautiful woman for whom a man will fight, steal, and journey far. We also see this image in the captivating, oft crowned goddesses with whom we, as magicians, converse and even assume into ourselves.

On the other hand, we also have numerous male characters who lack self-esteem and self-image, men with domineering mothers, nuns, sisters, and other women in their lives. It is less often that we see the male incorporate the Anima into himself, but this image is key to understanding some aspects of our magical ascent of the Qabalistic Tree.

Women and men both encounter this aspect of themselves in story, song, film, and within themselves throughout their lives. We often turn to the Animus/Anima for inspiration, for care that reminds us of childhood, for understanding of the other gender, and, ultimately, for integration into the self. In magick, we turn to this sense of other in the goddesses and gods, to broaden ourselves and our understanding of the cosmos, or to heal ourselves by seeking wholeness.

The Syzygy (Divine Couple)

The Syzygy is the unification or integration of the opposite sides of our natures. It is the integration of the Animus into the woman, or Anima into the man, achieving wholeness and balance. In magick, this is the principle of the two outer pillars of the

Qabalistic Tree—finding wholeness in the middle way. It is the Christ Child, the blending of the male and female principles into a powerful and balanced being of light. We see this image over and over in religion and sense it within ourselves. It is, in one way, a part of the regeneration of the Aurum Solis tradition.

Concerning the preceding archetypes, Jung wrote:

> ...I should like to emphasize that the integration of the shadow, or the realization of the personal unconscious, marks the first stage in the analytic process, and that without it a recognition of anima and animus is impossible. The shadow can be realized only through a relation to a partner, and anima and animus only through a relation to a partner of the opposite sex, because only in such a relation do their projections become operative. The recognition of the anima gives rise, in a man, to a triad, one third of which is transcendent: the masculine subject, the opposing feminine subject, and the transcendent anima. With a woman the situation is reversed.[3]

This process is very close to the process we observe in our progress along the path of initiation, regeneration, and aspiration to light. We will look at this statement from another perspective in chapter 11.

The Child

Jung postulated two more archetypes that are useful as magical tools: the Child and the Self.

The Child archetype is our constant hope for new beginnings, regeneration, and rebirth. It is paradise regained. Child images like the New Year's baby clearly derive from this archetype. The birth of the Christ Child or other spiritual being who unites heaven and Earth, human and God, is a powerful archetypal image driving many of the world's religions.

The Self

Jung postulated a grand archetype of human self-perception. For him, this was the image of the divine within. This is panentheism as a way of life. All is divine. All is spirit. This is the realization of the true self, the Higher Genius, the holy guardian angel.

The spirit descends upon Jesus in the wilderness as a dove. A voice declares you are my son, my beloved. This is an archetypal moment of true self. Galahad achieving the Grail and ascending with it to heaven is another drama of self. Lancelot's failure to achieve the Grail illustrates his failure to achieve the true self.

JOSEPH CAMPBELL: THE HERO'S JOURNEY

I wrote earlier of Joseph Campbell and his work in analyzing the myths and stories that form the foundations of human development and culture. You may already be familiar with Campbell's work through his landmark PBS series, *The Power of Myth*. In his explorations, Campbell was drawn to certain archetypes that recur in myth and story. He looked for those myths that were most popular, which most markedly captured the public imagination to such a degree that they were told over and over, from culture to culture, century to century.

Campbell explored an important archetype in these myths, one that has great bearing on the magical path. He expounded on his archetype in his book *Hero With a Thousand Faces: the Mythic Hero and the Hero's Journey.*

The Archetypal Mythic Hero

Campbell noticed that there was a typical sequence of actions attributed to heroic figures in myth. A legendary hero is usually the founder of a religion, city, philosophy, or other event or object that changes the course of a culture's development for the better. A hero is one who must leave his or her normal world in order to complete a journey or perform a task, someone who is willing to sacrifice his or her own needs on behalf of others. At root, the idea of hero is connected with self-sacrifice, self-denial, and transcendence through sacrifice.

Campbell postulated that the Hero, once identified in the myth, then followed a certain structure in completing the required journey or task. This structure he defined as the Hero's Journey:

Stage 1: Departure or Separation

    I.   World of Common Day
    II.   Call to Adventure
    III.   Refusal of the Call
    IV.   Supernatural Aid
    V.   Crossing the First Threshold
    VI.   Belly of the Whale

Stage 2: Descent, Initiation

    I.   Road of Trials

    II.   Meeting with the Goddess

    III. Woman as Temptress

    IV. Atonement with the Father

    V.   Apotheosis

    VI. The Ultimate Boon

Stage 3: Return

    I.   Refusal of the Return

    II.   The Magick Flight

    III. Rescue from Within

    IV. Crossing the Threshold

    V.   Return

    VI. Master of Two Worlds

    VII. Freedom to Live

Thinking over some of the common myths and stories of our own culture, it is not difficult to see most, if not all, of these stages in the journeys of our mythological heroes. From the labors of Hercules to *Star Wars,* this basic template can be placed over many stories to reveal their hidden structures. Moreover, this operation works just as well in reverse: this template can be used in the development of new stories, whether they are creations of literature or personal mythologies of spiritual attainment and journeys to adepthood.

VOGLER'S ARCHETYPES

One writer who has used this template to great advantage in the analysis of the mythology behind current films such as *Star Wars, Raiders of the Lost Ark, The Lion King,* and others is Christopher Vogler, author of *The Writer's Journey.*[4] Vogler proposed a modification of Campbell's original work that was adapted to the film industry and exemplified in the work of such filmmakers as George Lucas, Steven Spielberg, and Francis Ford Coppola.

Expanding on Campbell's work, Vogler found that, alongside the Hero, there are several other figures that recur in our greatest film and television stories. His work is important to the student of magick because these media are the new "campfires" around which our hearts are stirred with tales and song (though the Internet is beginning to challenge even the mighty television for public attention and entertainment).

Many come to the study of magick through the mythology presented in movies and on television, and this is far from a bad thing. While there is a snobbish cachet in declaring that all of television and film is little more than the visual equivalent of "junk food," as magicians, we find countless ideas, inspiration, images, and archetypal stories here. In science fiction, fantasy, historical drama, horror, and many other film genres we find much that is useful, provided that we are at least somewhat discriminating. On the other hand, there is a danger in this easy access to the storehouse of mythic images on television and other sources: Magick requires very real work, while television tends to lessen the motivation to pursue more active engagements. Balance, as in all things, is necessary.

Vogler suggested the following as primary archetypes in modern drama. I examine each with regard to its role in myth and modern story, and its implications for the magician.

The Hero

Vogler's Hero, in its mythical aspect, is essentially the same as Campbell's: self-sacrificing, but with an enormous ego. In psychological terms, the Hero is Freud's concept of ego. The journey of the Hero, through interior terrors and monsters, is the ego's journey of discovery and struggle toward completion and integration.

In magical terms, the Hero is you when you first start the study of the mysteries. It is the ego that drives you toward the goal. Yet, as we will see later, this Hero must die and be reborn for the goal to be reached. The path of magick is a search for wholeness and integration, for the discovery of the true and divine self, and the regeneration that brings full integration of this knowledge.

The Mentor: Wise Old Man or Woman

The Mentor is a figure who often appears in dreams or visions as someone or something that trains, prepares, initiates, or otherwise helps the Hero. In Campbell's work, this is the Wise Old Man or Wise Old Woman. Merlin, the fairy godmother, Obi Wan Kenobi, and Yoda are all typical of the Mentor. Mentors teach and often give important gifts to the Hero. In psychological terms, the Mentor is the inner self that guides us, the divine within.

In magick, the Mentor can be many things. For a time, the Mentor may be this book, or another text of magick or philosophy that guides you and fundamentally changes your outlook on life.

The Mentor may be a teacher, perhaps a more experienced magician, a leader of a group of magicians, or even an adept.

In the East, it is said that when the student is ready, a teacher will appear. This is true of magick, and of all life. Wisdom is found in many places. When found, it is best to allow it to lead you for a time while you determine what role this particular Mentor plays in your own journey. In your progress as a magician, your Mentor will change from time to time. Some will be better or more useful than others, yet each is necessary and serves a greater purpose. Seek out your mentors, and recognize them when they appear, for the readiness of the student depends on two things: the clarity to see the Mentor when he or she arrives, and the willingness to undergo the change in yourself that any Mentor will bring.

While the Mentor brings wisdom and guidance into our lives, however, there is a danger inherent in this relationship: an over-reliance of the student upon the Mentor. There is a tendency for many students of magick to treat their Mentors as gurus—that one teacher, one book, one interpretation of magick that becomes, for them the "True and Right Way." This is especially dangerous when the "True and Right Way" resides in a person. With all due respect to the great Eastern traditions, the difficulty inherent in their reliance on gurus is twofold:

1. Mentors only learn so much in their travels and work, and then only from their own perspective, colored by their own experience. Our Mentors' teachings reflect their own personal experiences and biases, and leave out anything they failed to learn in their own studies. Thus, no matter how celebrated and steeped in wisdom a Mentor appears to be, he or she can still only go so far with you on the way of

return. Eventually, the essence of the work is always between you and your soul.

2. Reliance on a Mentor leads you away from reliance on your own sense of the true self. To rely too much on another for such guidance only undermines the faith you must develop in your inner senses, and encourages the very sort of insecurities that are chief among the Threshold Guardians (see below). It is only through your sense of true self that you will find the guidance and wisdom needed to complete this journey. The light that brightens the way shines forth from your own heart.

Threshold Guardians

In myth, the Threshold Guardians are figures who test or otherwise menace the Hero as he or she moves into new realms or situations, often allowing only the "worthy" to pass. They are doorkeepers, bouncers, sentries, or soldiers, sometimes with a symbiotic relationship to a villain. In psychological terms, Threshold Guardians are neuroses, our internal demons, vices, weaknesses, and self-limitations. These hidden guardians within test us when we decide to try something new or to make a change in our lives.

Threshold Guardians will be quite familiar to students of magick. To a new student, the Guardian may be the difficulties life presents to test your perseverance in following the way of the mysteries. Family or friends may disapprove, or you may have difficulty making time for the study and practice required. You may find yourself struggling with doubts about the entire venture, gripped by moments of "reason" in which you decide that magick is all just a lot of nonsense. These are the guardians of the first gate on the path to light and regeneration. They are, while appearing entirely mundane, some of the most dangerous of all guardians, as we must transcend our usual tendency to give over to them the ability and power to prevent the discomfort of change.

Order documents tell us that

> the life of incarnate beings is continually subject to the ever-changing interplay and combat of abstract forces, which find their expression in embodied form. Our own bodies, our own mental and emotional faculties, take part in the contention; and, now in sport, now in grim earnest, convince us, if we need convincing, that to win peace and repose is no easy thing, but the fruit of the greatest victory of all.

To intermediate and advanced students of magick, the Threshold Guardians take another form. The realms beyond and within have very real guardians at the gates, assuring that none pass who are not ready, none enter but the worthy and prepared. There is no misleading these entities, no tricks or lies that may gain entry, as they exist on a plane quite apart from this one and can see quite clearly through misrepresentation and superficial preparation. This is entirely to our own benefit, however, as the gates defended by these guardians open to realms that can pose a great threat to the mental, emotional, and spiritual health of the unprepared and unready.

The Herald

The Herald is a figure who brings a challenge or proposes an adventure to the Hero. In Greek mythology, the Herald is Hermes, the messenger god. In *The Odyssey*, Hermes brings the message to Odysseus that allows him to defeat a witch (Threshold Guardian) who has turned his men into animals. Psychologically, the Herald is the inner call for change. It may come in a dream, a person, an idea, a book you just found, or a song you just heard. The Herald's message is clear: change.

In magick, the Herald is an inner sense, a call that appears in dreams and visions, in the corner of your vision, at the edge of your hearing, faint messages from your true self, a Higher Genius who attempts to communicate your True Will. To integrate the Herald into our being is the first step to finding your True Will, one of the highest goals of the Western mysteries. It is the beginning of the characteristic looking within of the adept.

Shapeshifters

In story, these characters often mislead the Hero by shifting in appearance or attitude. Shapeshifters are usually of the opposite sex, and are sometimes the love interest of the Hero. To Volger, Shapeshifters are the psychological equivalent of Jung's Anima/Animus.

Magically, Shapeshifters appear in many ways, both positive and negative. In their most important and beneficial guise, they represent the desire within for wholeness, for integration and recognition of that part of yourself that is opposite the gender of your birth. Your true self is genderless, appearing now male, now female. Most of us have already existed as both genders at one time or another. Sexual identity is a fundamental and vital part of the human mind, but that very human mind is little more than a mask worn by a self that is neither male nor female, but has the potential to be either. To find and integrate the Shapeshifter within—that elusive, shifting aspect of "other" (in gender terms) within us—is one essential step toward wholeness, and a step toward understanding what lies behind the mask.

The Shadow

Vogler's Shadow is essentially the same as Campbell's, the hidden side of the Hero, or parts of him/herself that the Hero has repressed or rejected. In story, the Shadow often appears as the villain, antagonist, or enemy.

Psychologically, Volger's Shadow represents repressed emotion and the great dark power something gains when we push it down out of our view. As the Threshold Guardians were the neuroses of the mind, the Shadow is the psychoses of the mind, the inner monsters that not only trouble and slow us, but may destroy us. In dreams, Shadows are our monsters, demons, vampires, and other powerful and frightening threats.

In magick, we face many demons, most not particularly troublesome. These strike us more as Threshold Guardians than as true enemies. The Shadow is what was called "The Dark Side" in *Star Wars*, that elusive, seductive, scary part of ourselves that we fear to claim, much less integrate. The thoughts and desires we most fear in ourselves, those that we push down quickly, those that challenge our idea of who we are—all these are the Shadow. Dark gods, goddesses, and demons are the Shadow. In magick, the Shadow may appear as a frightening astral image; in life, the Shadow may be unexamined thoughts and emotions relating to an abusive childhood or some other powerfully dark event in the life of the magician. All of these unexamined, repressed, and stagnant aspects of ourselves present dangers to the way of return.

The path of magick is a path of integration and wholeness, and the Shadow is part of that process. We work with Shadow entities to understand that side of ourselves we are afraid to claim. Ultimately, the Shadow must be integrated into the self to attain balance. Just as integrating the Anima or Animus achieves a balance between male and female, integrating the Shadow achieves a balance of light and dark.

There is a danger in the Shadow, however. There is great power and freedom in first accepting this side of ourselves. Students of magick often have a tendency to immerse themselves in the Shadow in a misguided attempt to understand it. Thus we have some magicians, tattooed with traditional symbols of death or evil, dressed in black, looking as "dark" as they possibly can, living for the shock value they give to those around them. These have accepted the Shadow, but only superficially. They will find no more magical success immersed in the Shadow than those who deny the Shadow. Further along this line are those who truly and fully embrace the Shadow, but we will say little of them here: the newspapers are filled with their sad tales. Unfortunately, most seem to believe in the rightness of what they have done, or do their dark deeds in the name of some righteous cause. As Vogler writes:

> It's important to remember...that most Shadow figures do not think of themselves as villains or enemies. From his point of view, a villain is the hero of his own myth,

and the [Hero] is his villain. A dangerous type of villain is "the right man," the person so convinced his cause is just that he will stop at nothing to achieve it. Beware the man who believes the end justifies the means. Hitler's sincere belief that he was right, even heroic, allowed him to order the most villainous atrocities to achieve his aims.[5]

The Shadow must be accepted and integrated, yet we need not act out the Shadow to know it. We need not commit the act we most fear to accept that this fear is within us. We need to look within and accept that which is there, bringing the Shadow into the light of consciousness, where it always loses much of its looming power. We must, as magicians, work with the Shadow entities we meet for what they are: a necessary balance to the manifested universe, expressions of a basic duality in creation, needed in the order of things.

The Trickster

Dramatically, Tricksters are those characters who embody mischief in the Hero's life, perhaps as a comic sidekick. This archetype can be combined with the Hero to become the Trickster Hero, a powerful archetype such as the coyote or raven in Native American thought, or the Fool of the tarot deck. In terms of psychology, the Trickster is our ability to laugh at ourselves, bringing about healthy change, bringing the Hero back to Earth.

Magically, Tricksters can be either parts of ourselves, or entities that we meet. As entities, elementals are a good example of magical Tricksters. These are playful entities with their own sense of the cosmos, who often delight in responding to a magician's bidding (see chapter 10). Yet frequently, elementals accomplish the required tasks in unintended ways, and often in ways that are downright amusing. Nancy Watson, in her book *Practical Solitary Magic*, related an interesting story about what happened after she made contact with Ondines, the elemental spirits of water.

> In the meantime, I started to have inundation dreams. Every night for a week, I dreamt that the monsoons had arrived and that my house had a roof like a sieve. The water crashed through the roof, ruining my house and all my furniture. I also developed a sinus condition. I dutifully made notes on all the dreams for my psychiatrist. Then one very rainy day, I was seated in a restaurant, snuffling and snorting and making notes on yet another inundation dream, and the light finally dawned. I had indeed made contact with the Ondines, and they were having their little joke at my expense. I knew that I should ask them to cease and desist. I also knew they were having too much fun to pay any attention to me.[6]

Watson then relates how she resolved this situation, but her story is typical of those who first contact elementals. Just as we are ever so impressed with our ability to contact an entity that comes from an entirely different realm, the entity in question bruises our glowing egos with playful jokes. Tricksters are necessary to the process of magick, and necessary parts of the universe. They are necessary to another task, as well: teaching the magician to take life and magick a little less seriously.

THE MAGICAL MYTHIC JOURNEY

Vogler proposed a modification to Campbell's Hero's journey, adapted to the contemporary hero story. His version is a useful model for the interpretation of many of our modern-day myths, but may also be used to understand the myth of the Solar Hero and the progress of the initiate on the magical path. As useful as this template may prove, however, remember that all of these images, templates, archetypal descriptions, and hero's progressions are merely keys with which to analyze your life and progress in the world of magick. Do not mistake the map for the road. Magick cannot be reduced to such simple terms, and the path will undoubtedly reveal itself as a vastly more complex and beautiful path of light as you progress in your study and work.

The Ordinary World

Most stories begin with a description of the Hero in his or her life before the heroic adventure begins. This is the part of the story that gives us a picture of a person that we ourselves just might know; someone who often has many of the same problems we have, and who is often just muddling along through life on an uneven course.

This character could be you, before you even knew that there was such a thing as magick, or rather after you forgot about the magick you took for granted in childhood. You may have picked up a few books, or found a few Web pages, or otherwise been exposed to the idea that there is something out there called magick, but seemed far away and something that others did.

The Call to Adventure

The call to adventure is the call the Hero receives that draws him or her away from normal life. In fact, the call is such that the Hero can no longer remain in the ordinary world. It sets the stakes and goals of the journey. With awareness of the goal, the Hero is sent on his or her way, impelled by a need from deep within.

For students of the mysteries, this is the moment when you have *that* dream, or read *that* book that strikes a chord within you, or have a chance meeting with someone who starts a process within you. Perhaps your call may come through small hints that have been there for years suddenly finding an outlet or a goal. The call is an experience that cannot be forgotten. You want to study magick. You need to study magick. Something greater than you has called you and the change it implies becomes a discordant feeling within you, pushing you, seeking some resolution. Perhaps, at this point, you buy many books on the subject, and begin reading philosophy and theology as well. Perhaps you seek out a magical order or working group. In any case, the call has been issued, been heard, and a response is demanded.

Refusal of the Call

The mythic Hero, having heard the call, often hesitates, or balks at the demands of the journey or the terms of the goal. Expressing anything from reluctance to outright refusal, the Hero clings to the ordinary world to avoid facing the fear that always accompanies the unknown. At this point, the Hero requires additional inducement to begin the journey. This is usually provided in the form of encouragement from a Mentor or some other dramatic change in circumstances.

The student of magick often hesitates as well, or even quits the study before really beginning it. Perhaps friends or family disapprove, or you feel they will disapprove. And there are just so many books out there, how could anyone ever read all this? And, of course, there is no time in your schedule for this after all. And why start something new anyway? Didn't you just give up that exercise program, that yoga class, or that pottery class at the local college? Many mundane issues can arise to drown out the call, sometimes accompanied by dreams consisting of your fears about the study of magick. There are risks, we know, and a part of us believes the fallacy that a risk-free life is a safe life.

The Mentor (The Wise Old Man or Woman)

At this point in most tales, the Hero meets a wise woman or Merlin-like person who becomes the Hero's Mentor, teacher, and guide. Sometimes the Mentor presents itself in the form of knowledge, perhaps a special book of knowledge; or a supernatural sponsor, as when Athena becomes the Mentor to Odysseus during his voyages across the sea. Often, the Mentor simply gets the Hero going, or provides tools or knowledge to start the journey. No matter how far the Mentor goes with the Hero, however, there must be an end to this relationship, for, at some point, the Hero must go alone into the unknown in pursuit of the goal. The relationship between hero and Mentor is one of the most common themes in mythology, and one of the richest.

In magick, the Mentor appears when the Hero has persevered through the mundane, and is acting in response to the call. Often, at this point, a Mentor will present itself in the form of a person, group, or book, giving direction and purpose to the first few steps along the magical path.

Crossing the First Threshold

At this point, in myth, the Hero boards the ship, climbs aboard the train, or simply gets moving, leaving the ordinary world behind. The Hero takes the first step into the realms beyond, into another, unknown world. The terms of the journey have been agreed upon, and the Hero is aware of the dangers, but can no longer resist the call to adventure.

In Aurum Solis, this is the point at which the aspirant has accepted the First Hall initiation, leaving behind the world as he or she has known it. As Order documents state,

> Before we proceed, know this. Whoso enters the Mysteries can nevermore return to the evening world of unenlightened selfhood. To take the first step upon the sacred Way of Return is to be committed to it for ever.

This is the crossing of a threshold from which there is no return.

One may remain in the outward life, still going to school or work, still having the same social calendar, still watching television in the evenings and seeing a film every Saturday night. Yet the person doing these things will never again see them the same way, and will never again be the person who did these things before. A catalyst has been placed into the core of the initiate, and the transformation it creates is already underway. The journey has begun!

Tests, Allies, and Enemies

Once across the first threshold, the Hero of the tale now encounters challenges that test his or her resolve. Driven to make or find allies and enemies, the Hero begins to learn the rules of this new world.

The initial study of magick is often somewhat disappointing to the new student. What seems the most interesting material requires the development of basic skills and acquisition of basic knowledge before it may be attempted. Adepthood is not just around the corner, but is a long and difficult journey that still lies ahead. Moreover, students of the mysteries, in learning basic skills, become aware that the world is not as they once believed. There is a much wider range of existence than they ever imagined. Virtually every assumption they had made about reality and the meaning of human existence is challenged. Many cross the first threshold, obtain the first initiation in a magical group, or perform a self-initiation, yet few continue to the next level. This is the test of your resolve; these are the challenges placed upon the road to test you.

Approach to the Inmost Cave

The mythic Hero, having faced tests and challenges, having made allies and overcome enemies, now comes to the edge of a dark and dangerous place, often underground or in a hidden or forgotten place. The most dangerous enemy often lives here, and the risks to the Hero are great. The Hero often pauses at this point, stopping at the gate, as it were, to plan and prepare.

In magick, the way of return is partly a matter of new experiences and knowledge, but it is also a matter of letting go of your assumptions about your world, about who you are. Some of your favorite ideas must be replaced with new ideas gained from the work and from experience. It is simply not possible to move along the magical way without changing, at the very core, who you believe yourself to be.

Knowing this, many hesitate before allowing change to happen. They "pause at the gate" to read more books, go over everything again, meet and talk with more magicians looking for guidance or reassurance. Some leave the study of magick altogether for a time, returning later when a sort of magical maturity allows them to approach this gate with less fear.

The Supreme Ordeal

Having crossed into the inmost cave, entered the gate, made the descent, the Hero is locked in battle with his or her greatest fear. This is a life-and-death struggle, and often the prospects for the Hero do not look good. This is a dark moment in the story, as the Hero must face the distinct possibility of death. It is often at this point that the Hero either dies or appears to die, making way for rebirth. Every heroic adventure needs such a life-and-death moment, an essential element in the age-old drama of death and rebirth of the Solar Hero.

In Aurum Solis, death and rebirth of the Solar Hero is the process begun with the Second Hall rite of integration. The initiate must have developed the ability to call on the ethereal self, the astral self, which is involved in this rite. That which is negative and vain in initiates and their world is exorcised and banished. A part of the initiates is put away forever, cut loose to drift away. Initiates are then blessed with light and started on the next stage of the journey. The exorcism and banishment of that which is negative, destructive, and vain is a death of sorts—a part of the ego dying under the will of the conscious aspiration for Light. The effects of this rite can be dramatic in the life of the initiate, magically and psychologically.

Reward (Seizing the Sword)

The mythic Hero has survived a close brush with death, or died and been reborn. Having conquered the greatest fear, the Hero now takes the reward or goal, often a magick sword, a holy object, or some special elixir to heal a wounded land or people. Sometimes, the reward is special knowledge, a special language, or a new perspective that can be brought back to redeem a land or people.

In magical terms, the initiate, having come to terms with the effects of the rite of integration, may now begin to study the deep mysteries of the order and begin the search for the goal or reward. At this point, the initiates hone their basic skills, while learning new advanced techniques and wrestling with difficult philosophical ideas, all while learning to look within for answers, learning to trust the divine self within.

The Road Back

The mythic journey is not yet finished, as the Hero begins to deal with the consequences of confronting the dark forces of the supreme ordeal. Yet the dark forces are not entirely defeated. They have only escaped, and may send forces raging after the Hero in search of revenge, or to finish the job started in the earlier life-and-death struggle. Often, the Hero is chased or pursued at this point, the dark forces of the supreme ordeal wanting to recover the stolen sword or elixir. This stage marks the decision to return to the ordinary world. The Hero knows that the journey must have an end, and that the half-way point has been reached. Of course, dangers, temptations, and challenges lie ahead.

At this point, the initiate of the mysteries has come far, and learned many skills. A certain wisdom and maturity have been achieved, along with a willingness to undergo a true rebirth in light and wisdom. Moreover, the initiate has honed many skills and looked deeply within, finding there a yearning for something just out of reach, something that, for the first time, has become a very real presence at the very core of her or his soul: the Higher Genius and the knowledge of the True Will.

Resurrection

In ancient times, hunters and warriors were purified before returning to their villages. The blood on their hands and bodies, the blood of the hunt, made them impure and unsuited for the peaceful life of the village. Symbolic death and rebirth was a common characteristic of these rituals. At this point, the Hero, who has been to the realm of the (unclean) dead must be reborn and cleansed. This usually occurs in the form on one last ordeal of death and rebirth or resurrection.

Likewise, the initiate Order now present themselves for the Third Hall Rite of Elevation, a dramatic ritual of death and rebirth, a final release of the illusions of selfhood and separateness. In this rite, the initiate steps forward, master of his or her skills, and moving comfortably and effectively through the magical world. The journey is far from over, but much work has been done, and the initiate is ready to rise from the dramatic death in the rite as a being reborn, robed in light, with keys to access parts of the universe only dimly imagined before. Much is revealed at this time, as the former initiate now steps forward as an Alchemist of Spirit, the Adept.

The Adept is master of her or his own universe, with but a single task left to accomplish: to find the Higher Genius within and, through this contact, to discover the True Will. The time of mentors and guides is over. The Adept must seek this final balance, this union of inner and outer, alone.

Return with the Elixir

The mythic hero returns to the ordinary world, but the risks and trials of the journey are wasted unless he or she brings back the treasure, the elixir, or the valued lesson from the spiritual realms. The elixir may be a great treasure, the Holy Grail for example, with the power to heal a wounded land or people. It may take the form of love, freedom, wisdom, or simply the knowledge and experience that a special world exists and that other journeys are possible. Often, all of this is merely one cycle in a larger tale, such as the twelve labors of Hercules.

The elixir of the adept is the Higher Genius and the True Will. Having discovered this, the Adept may return to his or her life, but he or she will never be the same, nor see life the same. Many things come with adepthood, and many more with the discovery of the Higher Genius and True Will. The Adept may now walk in the world of the unawakened, serving as a beacon, becoming, in this way, the Hermit of the tarot, leading by light, inspiring by example.

The very presence of an adept in your life may trigger the call that sets you on this same wondrous path of regeneration and return.

CONTACT WITH THE ARCHETYPAL WORLD

The first formal ritual studied at Lapis Lazuli is the Calyx. The Calyx is one of the most fundamental tools of Art Magick, bringing you in contact with the cosmos and leading you to find the links to the cosmos within yourself. Remember, we are not separate from the vast realms around us; it only appears as if we are. This rite has many uses, and may be used often. It serves admirably as a psychic toner or warm-up. It may be used as a form of adoration of the light, or as a preparatory rite to set the stage for workings of power. This rite, while easy to learn and simple to apply, should not be underestimated in its importance to the practice of Art Magick, nor in its long-term benefits to the practitioner. All the rites of Art Magick may be visualized as a pyramid, upside down. The point of the pyramid is this rite, the Calyx.

It should be mentioned, as well, that *calyx* is the Greek word for cup or chalice. It is so named because, to accomplish the drawing down of divine light that is the fundamental aspect of this rite, one must be a receptive vessel, putting aside the mundane self for the greater magical self.

The Calyx
1. Face east, assume the wand posture. Vibrate: **EI (EI)**
2. Raise your arms at your sides, gently, until they are almost horizontal, but relaxed, palms facing up. (This is known as the Tau posture.) Vibrate: Η ΒΑΣΙΑΕΙΑ **(HE BASILEAI)**
3. Touch your right shoulder with your left palm. Vibrate: ΚΑΙ

Η' ΔΨΝΑΜΙΣ **(KAI HE DUNAMIS)**

4. Touch your left shoulder with your right palm. Vibrate: KAI Η' ΔΟΞΑ **(KAI HE DOXA)**

5. Bow your head. Vibrate: ΕΙΣ ΤΟΥΣ ΑΙΟΝΑΣ **(EIS TOUS AIONAS)**

Notes for the Calyx

1. Begin by establishing the rhythmic breath. Visualize a tongue of flame above your head, representing the Higher Genius and the sacred flame of magick. Hold this image in your mind. When you breathe out, vibrate: **EI**

2. As you breathe in, raise your arms to Tau, palms up, as if opening yourself to the divine powers above. Sense Jupiter, the principle of mercy, on the left, Mars, the principle of strength, on the right. Breathe out. On the next inhalation, visualize a shaft of brilliant light passing from the flame, through the center column of your body to the ground between your feet. Release the breath and vibrate: **HE BASILEIA**

3. On inhalation, bring the palm of your left hand to your right shoulder and acknowledge the forces of Mars at the right. Release the breath and vibrate: **KAI HE DUNAMIS**

4. On inhalation, bring the palm of your right hand to your left shoulder and acknowledge the forces of Jupiter at the left. Release the breath and vibrate: **KAI HE DOXA**

5. Keep your arms crossed, right over left. At the end of the next breath, pause and lower your head. Feel the shaft of light within, radiating energy, warmth, and light into your being. Feel a great concentration of light and power at your

heart center, in your breast (not your solar plexus). Release the breath and vibrate: **EIS TOUS AIONAS**

Perform this rite frequently, at least once each day. With time, the visualizations will increase in clarity and your magical senses will sharpen. What seems a simple rite today will grow in strength and usefulness to you over time. Beginning students and adepts alike perform the Calyx in one form or another each day, and have for centuries. There are corresponding rites in other traditions— Hebrew, Christian, and Moslem—a similar drawing down of divine light occurring daily in temples, monasteries, and private worship around the world. Each time you perform this rite, know that you are connecting with the echoes of everyone in our tradition who has ever performed the Calyx, joining in sympathetic vibration with all those who similarly draw light into our world.

8

Banishments, Warding, and Astral Defenses

E very magical tradition teaches the concept of astral defenses. In the course of Aurum Solis study, students learn several forms of this, increasing in complexity and strength. Why set up astral defenses? The very word "defense" or "banishment" almost implies that you are under some sort of attack. While magical acts do attract the attention of unpleasant energies from time to time, the principle value of these rites lies in defining a space for magical activities and quieting the astral and energetic influences so encircled. The principle of defense is important as well, and the dangers are not to be ignored. Yet, as you learn to fill a space with light, there will be little room for anything else. The several Aurum Solis rites known collectively as the Setting of the Wards focus both on clearing a space of unwanted influences and bringing desired influences into that space.

With more advanced magical activities, the issue of astral defenses becomes critical, for, as magicians delve more deeply into other realms, they will find that not everything out there is friendly or pleasant. At this point in your studies, you should begin the regular performance of a rite that starts to accumulate defenses that will aid you in future work.

Below is the Lapis Lazuli Circle of Light, a ritual used even by the advanced magicians of Lapis Lazuli when a quick Warding rite is desired. This is a very useful rite that clears a circular space of undesired influences and draws a circle of light around you. This rite, or one that accomplishes the same purpose, should be performed before all acts of magick, astral travel, and deep meditation. On a practical basis, the Circle of Light is useful simply to quiet down the psychic air around you, creating a peaceful temple in the midst of a chaotic world.

The Lapis Lazuli Circle of Light

1. Stand at the center of the space, facing east.
2. Perform the Calyx.
3. Visualize a ray of white light emanating from the flame (established in the Calyx) above you.
4. This light becomes a spiral descending around you, counterclockwise, disappearing into the ground at your feet.
5. Allow this visualization to fade from your consciousness.
6. Extend your arms in front of you, slightly elevated, with palms facing outward.
7. With the visualization of the flame above you firmly in mind, turn in place, counterclockwise, 360 degrees. As you turn, visualize a wall of light beyond your palms, white with golden sparkles, spreading as your hands move, to encircle the place of your working. Finish by completing the circle and facing east once again.
8. Lower your arms and turn counterclockwise to face west. Raise your arms over your head, palms out, and firmly

stamp once with your right foot, while proclaiming the words: **PROCUL ESTE, PROFANI!**[1]

9. As you proclaim the banishing charge, know that, through the strength and authority of your Higher Genius, through your magical self, you are banishing all undesirable and unbalanced forces from your circle.

10. Fold your arms on your chest, right over left, and imagine a clear and empty space around you, all impure forces being gone from it. The very air will change, feeling cooler and cleaner.

11. Turn counterclockwise to face east. Again raise your arms as before, palms out. With awareness of the flame above firmly in mind, turn clockwise, 360 degrees. As you turn, visualize a wall of light, mist-blue with silver sparkles, spreading as your hands move, to encircle the place of your working. Finish the turn, completing the circle and facing east once again.

12. Repeat the Calyx.

13. Finish the rite by folding your arms over your chest, left over right. Standing this way, reaffirm your visualizations of the flame above you and the mist wall around you. Feel the magical energy of the place of light you have just created.

This space is now prepared for rites of Art Magick such as the Attunement of the Robe of Art.

9

THE MAGICAL ROBE

The custom of wearing special clothing for ritual purposes has existed as long as there have been rituals—from the painted bodies and faces of ancient shamanistic rites, to the elaborate robes of magicians, priests, and others. Before the performance of the Catholic Mass, the officiating priest puts on specific pieces of clothing with great reverence and care, knowing that, as the cloth falls across his shoulders, he is transformed from a mere priest to a channel for the divine. Indeed, over time, all ritual clothing picks up the vibrations of use and the very fabric attunes itself to the habitual application. Ritual clothing helps us step out of our mundane, day-to-day selves and into a sacred self. It helps make the transition from one mode of thinking to another, one mood to another, one perspective to another, one mask of self to another.

The magical robe, known in Aurum Solis as the Robe of Art, is the first concrete step in the development of your magical personality. As noted in Order documents, the Robe of Art is a proclamation to the external universe and, more particularly, to the subliminal faculties of the operator, that a special work is about to be accomplished. Moreover, it conveys to the wearer that the everyday personality has given way to the magician—the person of power who is now to perform this special work.

The Robe of Art enfolds you, clothes you, hides you, and announces your true self each and every time you put it on. Therefore, the Robe of Art should be treated with care and reverence. Put it on only after you have appropriately calmed your thoughts and centered them on the profound symbolism of the act. The Robe of Art is not a costume; it is a sign of the true personage, the magician, of the deepest and finest aspects of your self. The robe enlarges you, sanctifies you, and clothes you for travel to other times and realms. It prepares you to step into the presence of the divine.

Whenever possible, the Robe of Art should be worn during most magical ritual activities. You should perform the Setting of the Wards fully robed at least once a week to help accustom yourself to this physical act of clothing the magical self. You should wear no clothing under the robe, though circumstances do sometimes dictate that you put the robes on over your street clothes.

You may either go barefoot or choose appropriate footware. If you choose to cover your feet, either sandals or soft shoes may be worn, as long as they are comfortable, secure upon your foot, and make little or no distracting noise when you move in them. Soft canvas Kung Fu shoes are ideal (and quite inexpensive), as are Roman sandals. Your Robe of Art should have a plain hood, large enough to completely hide your face and create darkness for yourself. Remember, to draw the hood over your face is not an act of hiding from the outer; it is a profound act of turning to the inner.

There is an interesting issue that students have mentioned to me. Students often feel a sensual or even sexual stirring within themselves as the robe envelopes them. This is a normal response. The stirring of the magical current is closely related to the sexual current. You may think of this sensation as the stirring of kundalini energy, or the uncoiling of the serpent that lies at the core of the magical self. In any case, do not let this sensation disturb you, and remember: There is nothing nonmagical or unspiritual about sensuality or sexuality. The sexual current, so deeply a part of every human being, is, at least partly, the impulse to seek the divine. The goal in magick is to learn to channel this energy into your ritual work, along with the other energies you raise or channel.

Weaving the Magick: The Lapis Lazuli Robe

First, let it be known that nowhere in the Aurum Solis traditional documents is there a consecration or blessing ceremony given for the Robe of Art. If you read more widely in magical literature, you will find that few magical texts mention the robe, beyond advising the aspirant to obtain one and wear it. Even in the Roman Catholic tradition, which has a holy consecration for almost every tool used in the Mass, the priest's robes are store-bought and hardly given a second thought before use.

Yet, over the years, I have found that any tool or item of clothing to be brought into the circle benefits from a formal process to bring the item from the mundane world into our sacred space.

At the Lapis Lazuli Commandery, we designate a particular robe, the shape and color of which is characteristic of our Commandery. As each new member creates this Robe of Art, each performs an individual Rite of Attunement to align the robe with his or her magical self. This rite, Attuning the Robe of Art, weaves the energy of magick into the ritual clothing. I present this rite here, and highly recommend it to the solitary practitioner of Art Magick as well.

ELEMENTS OF RITUAL

Before I describe the rite, I would like to refer to a portion of Marion Zimmer Bradley's *Mists of Avalon*. In this passage, she writes of the creation of a scabbard for the sword Excalibur.

> All that day, in silence, she worked, gazing into the chalice, letting the images rise...so wrapped in the magical silence that every object on which her eyes gazed, every movement of her consecrated hands, became power for the spell...She worked into the crimson velvet the signs of the magical elements of earth and air and water and fire...it seemed that needle and thread moved through her own flesh or through the flesh of the land, piercing earth and sky and her own blood and body...sign upon sign and symbol upon symbol...By sunset of the third day it was finished, every inch of the scabbard covered with twining symbols, some of which she did not even recognize; surely they had come directly from the hand of the Goddess through her hands? She lifted it...then said aloud, breaking the ritual silence, "It is done."[1]

There are several important features in the above extract that make the action described an excellent model for the development of a powerful rite of attunement to magical purpose. The Robe of Art is the first object to which you will apply such a focus of energy and magical will, so let us begin with an examination of the elements involved.

Intent

In all ritual work, we must first establish our intent, and decide which forces are involved or must be drawn into the rite. We must be sure that we have a connection to or relationship with the forces we have chosen, and that we have mastered that relationship to the degree that the forces of the rite may be called into our intent.

Morgaine does these things earlier in the chapter from which I quote, beginning when she is asked by Viviane to create the scabbard for this sword of legend and myth, a sword to be carried by a king. Morgaine prepares herself for this task and is led to a holy place suitable for such an important magical rite. She is clear about her intent, and knows what must be done. She identifies the energies of the working:

> ...she tried to remember that she was only a vessel of power and not the power itself, that the power itself came from the Goddess...[2]

Materials

The second principle is one of physical preparation. All things needed in the rite must be provided for, and any consecrated or sacrificial items must be in place. The Chamber of Art is prepared, containing only those symbols, colors, and items that are part of the rite, that serve to further the focus of the person conducting the operation. These may include incense, music, or other materials that further involve our senses in the rite.

As she began her seclusion, Morgaine used the sword itself to cut the fabrics and leather needed to make the sheath. She set aside the needed tools: needle and thread of gold and silver. She was attended by priestesses who provided her with food and water. She filled a chalice with water from a holy well, and this became her scrying bowl. All things in place, she began to seek the trance state she would need to accomplish the work.

Ritual Silence

Next among these important principles is the ritual silence. Any work of this type requires almost total concentration on the task at hand, a complete balancing of the self between two worlds, channeling threads of vision and energy from one world to the other as we work our influence into the weaving of the manifest world. This cannot be done with less than complete dedication to the task and seriousness of purpose. It cannot be done against the background noise of everyday life. It cannot be accomplished with periodic interruption.

Imagine, if you will, sitting in a movie theater watching a film, one that engrosses and fully involves you and your emotions. Imagine now that the person sitting next to you nudges you every few minutes to discuss some point unrelated to the film, and your enjoyment of the soundtrack is punctuated by a baby crying in the seat behind you. Do these distractions not take away from your ability to immerse yourself in the flow of the film and the lives of the characters? In a rite in which you provide the film, the projector, the theater, and the audience, concentration becomes vastly more difficult.

Many rites of magick require this type of silence, a formal separation of yourself from the mundane world. Of course, magical silence does not include words or chants used in the rite. It refers to outside influences that might distract from your purpose, and sounds that are not harmonious to the working or otherwise related by correspondence or inspiration.

The Offering

Next is the element of offering and self-sacrifice. Morgaine did this by limiting her diet to only water and bits of dried fruit. In this, there are two principles at work:

- First, food is grounding. A full meal grounds the work just as surely as a lead weight. In fact, after psychic work or astral travel, food is a very useful and enjoyable method to ground the activity and close off the energy. From this principle, the practice of following group ritual with feasts may have developed. Thus, while food after the rite is good and useful, meals before a rite should be avoided.
- Second, lack of food creates an emptiness, a yearning, and this yearning may easily be channeled in other directions. The self-denial of hunger is a sacrifice, one that opens channels of force and creates an emptiness that may be filled. Thus, it is also useful that the food taken during ritual not be part of the normal diet, for we seek to separate our mundane and magical selves.

Food and drink are among the oldest and most basic tools of ritual. The wine and wafers of Catholic Mass are not foods of this world, either by nature or by preparation. Over the course of many centuries, temples have served as storehouses of food for the gods. Religions have made strict rules about what may and may not be eaten during the rites of their gods.

The Work of the Rite: Rhythm and Rhyme

The paragraph quoted earlier has a hypnotic, repetitive quality in the description of the stitching. What begins simply as a physical act of sewing quickly becomes the vehicle for a profoundly altered state. The same can be true of voiced chants and incantations, but we must give some thought to how such chants should be constructed. Simple affirmations will not do. On this matter of creating suitable rhythmic chants for a ritual, I quote from Nancy Watson's advice on creating magical incantations in her *Practical Solitary Magic:*

> The best-known magical incantation in the English language is from Shakespeare's *MacBeth.* Act Four, Scene One opens with three witches, bent on serious mischief, stirring up a poisonous brew containing (for starters) Eye of newt and toe of frog, Wool of bat and tongue of dog, Adder's fork and blindworm's sting. They incant as they stir the pot: Double, double, toil and trouble; Fire burn, and caldron bubble.
>
> ...Please note that Shakespeare's witches don't go on and on about their intention. The don't say, for instance, We want to create a lot of toil and trouble in the lives of those who come into contact with us and in order to do this we are putting some thoroughly nasty

ingredients into our cauldron and....They keep it short.[3]

Almost every incantation that has been carried down to us through history has had a strong elements of both rhythm and rhyme.

In the passage from *Mists of Avalon*, the character, in the midst of her work, allows herself to become lost in the movements of her hands. Her vision focuses on a river of magical symbols and correspondences. It is while in this trance state that she loses herself entirely for a time, and goes so far as to create symbols that come directly from the hand of the Goddess. This is one type of trance state that is of enormous value in magical work.

Completion: The Quintessence

At the end of the third day, Morgaine breaks the magical silence and seals the rite with the words, "It is done." Once this silence is broken and the trance is lost, she finds herself exhausted, hungry, and feeling sick. It is a side-effect of a 72-hour rite like this one[4] that we can become so involved in the focus, intent, and power of the rite that time passes without us noticing our physical bodies. Indeed, this often happens during much shorter rites and meditations as well, though to a far lesser extent.[5]

The Lapis Lazuli

Attunement of the Robe of Art

For the Attunement of the Robe, we will adhere closely to the three basic ideas above: ritual silence, sacrifice, and incantation. The ritual should take place over the three days immediately preceding the Full Moon, or as close to this as possible. In no case should the three-day cycle extend past the day and hour of the Full Moon. That is to say, the three-day rite may end a day or two before the Full Moon if necessary, but it may not end the day after the Full Moon.

Preparation

1. Schedule three days just before the time of the Full Moon in which you will be able to follow through, without fail, the sunrise and sunset Solar Adorations, at least one Setting of the Wards each day, and one additional ritual specifically oriented to the Robe of Art.

2. Fill a small clean container with water. Use the purest water you can conveniently obtain, though tap water will do. Set aside a piece of bread, one that is fresh the day before your three-day rite. Unleavened breads are best, and pita bread is excellent for this purpose.

3. Finally, you will need thread the same color as the cloth of your robe, and a sewing needle.

The First Day

1. Begin the day with the morning Solar Adoration. Do this slowly, with meaning and attention to the symbolism of the adoration. Do not eat breakfast this day, though tea and fruit juices are acceptable.

2. Later that morning, at any time after the adoration, but before noon, take your robe, thread, needle, water, and bread to your Chamber of Art or another private place.

Place the items on your Bomos or upon the ground (on a cloth) and clear the area of negative influences with the Circle of Light rite.

3. When you have completed the circle, sit or stand, facing east, with the items in front of you. Tear off and eat one piece of the bread. Take one drink of the water. As you swallow these morsels of ritual food and drink, relax and let them serve as catalysts within you, meditating briefly on the symbolism of these materials and whatever personal meaning they have for you.

4. Thread the needle and locate an inner, hidden part of your robe, preferably at or near the waist.

5. Use the needle and thread to make seven loose stitches in the material, representing the heptagram and the planetary powers. If you like, you may place small beads on the thread with each stitch, but be certain that these beads are small, quite smooth, and nonmetallic.

6. As you make the first stitch, chant three times:

Star, Planets, Seven Lights
Truly bring this cloth to Life.

As you make each of the seven stitches into the cloth, repeat the incantation three times as a quiet chant. Relax, and let yourself be swept up in the rhythms of the chant and the work of needle. Make as many stitches and repetitions of the chant as necessary to achieve some measure of the state described above. It does not matter whether you achieve this state for seconds or minutes, but you must attempt to reach it.

7. When you have finished the seven stitches, repeat the chant as you fold the Robe of Art and place it before you.

8. Fall silent and reach out with your inner senses to feel the energy of the rite. Now say with confidence: **It is done.**

9. Close the ritual with the Calyx, and put the materials in a place where they will remain undisturbed and untouched.

10. For the remainder of the day, go about your normal affairs, and feel free to break your morning fast with a midday meal. End this day with the evening Solar Adoration, taking into yourself a fullness of the principle the Sun represents. Note in writing any dreams you may have that night.

The Second Day

1. Begin this day with the morning Solar Adoration as before. Eat a very light breakfast, but do not eat the midday meal.

2. In the afternoon of this day, gather your materials and go again to your Chamber of Art or another private place. Open the rite as before.

3. Thread the needle and find an inner part of your robe near the bottom, perhaps in the hem.

4. This time, make five stitches into the cloth, representing the pentagram and the elemental powers. Again, you may place small beads on the thread with each stitch, but be certain that these beads are small, quite smooth, and nonbreakable, as they may be caught underfoot during a rite.

5. As you begin the first stitch, chant three times:

> **Air, Fire, Water, Earth**
> **Truly bring this cloth to birth**

With each stitch, repeat the incantation three times as a quiet chant as before, once again seeking a meditative, altered state.

6. When you have finished the five stitches, repeat the chant as you fold the Robe of Art and place it before you.

7. Fall silent and reach out with your inner senses to feel the energy of the rite. Now say with confidence: **It is done.**

8. Close the ritual with the Calyx, and put the materials in a place where they will remain undisturbed and untouched.

9. For the remainder of the day, go about your normal affairs, and break your fast with a late afternoon snack. Freely partake of an evening meal. End this day with the evening Solar Adoration, taking into yourself a fullness of the principle the Sun represents. Note in writing any dreams you may have that night.

The Third Day

1. Begin this day with the morning Solar Adoration, as on the previous two days. Eat a light breakfast and midday meal; fast from midday until midnight. Perform the evening Solar Adoration at the setting of the Sun.

2. In the evening of this last day, under the fullness of the Moon, take the materials to your Chamber of Art or another private place, preferably outdoors. Prepare the place as before.

3. Thread the needle and find an inner part of your robe near the neckline, hood, or at the point of the hood.

4. This time, place eight stitches in the cloth, representing the Ogdoadic tradition and the Ogdoadic star of regeneration.

You may place small beads on the thread with each stitch, but be aware that if these stitches are near the neckline, beads may chafe and cause undesirable irritation during rites.

5. As you begin the first stitch, chant three times:

Lord, Lady, Holy Serpent
Bring to Strength This Mighty Garment

With each stitch, repeat the incantation three times as a quiet chant, again seeking an altered state.

6. When you have finished the eight stitches, continue the chant as your fold the Robe of Art and place it before you.

7. Fall silent and stay quietly in this state for a while, noting what thoughts, sounds, or visions come to you. These may be important later, so remember them and write them down after the ritual. Now, say with confidence: **It is done.**

8. Close the ritual with the Calyx, and place the materials where they will remain undisturbed and untouched until morning.

9. For the remainder of the evening, go about your normal affairs, and break your fast with a late evening snack. Note again any dreams you have that night.

After the Rite

Your robe is now a part of your magical self. It forms both an outer concealment, and the robe and sign of your magical personality. Wear your robe regularly during all formal rites of magick. You will begin to find that it develops an energetic affinity to you, picking up the magical energy of your workings. Begin wearing the Robe of Art for your daily magical work as well, such as Setting of Wards and meditations. Most important, when you put on your robe, know that you are a magician, a person of true power whose seat is in the cosmos and who is filled with light.

Note: The basic structure of this rite (and the fictional rite quoted earlier) is one found throughout Aurum Solis rites and other Western mystery traditions. It is known as the pattern of the House of Sacrifice. Ritual design is advanced work, but students at any level should be familiar with the basic principles outlined above. You will see them at work in many magical rituals that you may read from the various magical traditions. They will be of great use later in your explorations of the Ogdoadic tradition.

10

SOPHIA TERRAE

T he human mind has a tendency to categorize the world, and, as long as it is understood that these categories are little more than symbolic maps to a much greater whole, this tendency is one that has led to advancement in every field of human endeavor. From the time we are small children, we are taught to divide our world into animal, vegetable, and mineral, and this first categorization in fact becomes the basis for the first question in the game of 20 Questions.[1] Even before this three-part view of the world is taught, small children make their own categories into which they group the objects in their experience. Throughout the world and from the dawn of human consciousness, our presence on Earth has been an unending process of naming and grouping all that we see, hear, touch or imagine.

THE FOUR ELEMENTS

One of the earliest attempts at dividing the world into logical groups came with a recognition of four elements within nature.

These were not seen to be scientific principles as much as divine spirits, streams, and currents underlying all things.

These elements have been named and numbered in many different ways around the world, some traditions declaring three elements, some four, some five. Yet each culture and tradition has experienced the movement of divine energies in the material world and sought to describe them. Since these systems are all little more than maps of a greater realm, cultural differences are not particularly important, in the sense that one tradition is correct while another is wrong. A map may orient north, south, east, and west in any number of ways, as long as the map reader knows the relationship between north on the map and magnetic north.

Each tradition makes contact with its own energetic current, developing its own ideas of how the world is arranged according to a particular cultural perception of that current. Chinese fire is a powerful and authentic current leading to grand works of Taoist magick, martial art development, and almost the whole of Chinese medicine. It is neither lesser nor greater than the fire of the Western mysteries— merely different. Yet much of Chinese and Taoist thought and culture must be understood and integrated to make use of their elements. For this reason, as students of magick, we will concern ourselves primarily with a particular set of elements arising from ancient traditions—the building blocks of nature around us as perceived and developed through aeons by the mystery schools of the West.

These great classic symbols of magical force are four in number: air, earth, fire, and water. Each is a moving stream of spiritual force and life, not a static substance. They are never truly apart from one another, but are intermixed and intertwined throughout our world, giving their balance to all that exists. Because of this intermingling, the task of the magician is to learn to discern each elemental aspect, even where they are not apparently separable. Order documents tell us that

> this is essential, for when the elements are not separated they must be balanced; this cannot be left to chance, and the will of the magician in this respect is traditionally represented by his use of the four Elemental Weapons, as they are called. By the Wand, he rules the element of Fire; by the Cup, the element of Water; by the Dagger, the element of Air; and by the Pentacle, the element of Earth.

In addition to the attribution of a magical weapon to each element, there are two more correspondences that are of particular interest:

- The first relates to the attribution of the four-lettered Hebrew name of God, Yod Heh Vau Heh. In chapter 6, we attributed these characters to the active principle (yang), the passive principle (yin), balance (Tao), and manifestation (Qi), respectively. Antoher traditional attribution of these Hebrew letters is to the four elements: fire, water, air, and earth. The exploration of the interrelationships between the Taoist and Elemental attributions can be of great value to the student of the Western mysteries.[2]
- The second relates to an ancient quaternary known as the Four Virtues of the Hermeticist:

To Will

To Dare   To Know

To Keep Silent

Each of these virtues, which together comprise the nature of the magician, has an elemental correlation: to will is the heat, activity, and desire of fire; to dare is part of the airy intellectual realms of air; to know is to know and understand oneself from the dark depths of water; to keep silent is the silence of the great stones of earth. Meditation and exploration of these attributions will also prove of great value to the student.

The Aurum Solis magical tradition is more focused on the seven planets and the twelve signs of the zodiac than upon the four elements, yet this model is of great importance in understanding the other. The elemental weapons of the magician are only useful to this end.[3]

Moreover, the importance of the elements in understanding our own lives cannot be underestimated, for the elements are life. The human being is a microcosm of the greater universe and nature. That which flows through the cosmos flows through us.[4] All thinking, feeling, and action are in accordance with nature, and nature is in accordance with even greater laws. At any moment, we may look around us and within us and feel these elements, directly experiencing them. Over time, it is even possible to begin to see the movements of the lifeforms of the elements energizing and animating nature around us and within us.

CORRESPONDENCES: THE LAW OF SIMILARS

Since each of these four elements is actually a concept, a stream, an archetype, it remains for us to see how this root image is expressed around us, both in this world and beyond. One way to do this is to compile lists of correspondences, list of things that instruct us, remind us, or inspire us through the root image. Such lists are not meant to give a comprehensive definition of the outgrowth in the cosmos of a given element. However, once we have looked at enough different kinds of things that are associated with the root image of water, for example, we begin to gain a deeper knowledge of the archetype itself. From such knowledge, the stream of manifestation from archetype to lower plane may be divined and ways to work with these streams are revealed.

The development of correspondences follows an ancient principle, the Law of Similars. This is actually quite a simple law, stating that objects, energies, or entities that are similar in action, view, or other aspects, are related. Moreover, it claims that, through contact with one object, energy or entity, it becomes possible to make contact with another, and thus make contact with the root images behind both. Much of early medicine and modern homeopathy is based upon this very principle.

We actually use the Law of Similars in our lives quite frequently without ever knowing it. A few examples:

- You are watching a sporting event on television. As your favorite team is about to win or lose, you become progressively more interested and involved in the events, until you find that your body is tensing and moving in concert with the happenings on the television. One player rushes to score a point. You lean to the left when you see he must go left, lean forward as he gets closer to the goal, and, when the point is scored, you share some of the player's elation at his accomplishment.

- Someone near you drops a heavy object on his or her toe. You cringe, almost feeling the pain, though you are perfectly safe and at a distance from the mishap.

- As a child, you are taught that red is hot. You see a glowing red stove and touch it to find it is indeed hot. While not all reds are hot, your brain quickly works out a scheme for determining hot things using the color red as a key. When drawing a picture of something hot, you want to show others that the object is hot, so you color it red.

- You see a large, four-legged, brown animal eating grass in a field and you ask what it is called. A cow, you are told. Later, when speaking to another person you mention that you saw a cow in the pasture. This creates a picture in that person's thoughts, which you then complete by mentioning that the cow was brown, and was in a field and eating grass. Each piece of information brings the image of "cow" closer and closer in each of your minds.

Each of these events is a simple act of practical sympathetic magick. You have most likely been doing it most of your life. The goal of the magician is to learn to control these acts, plan them, and execute them in a way that leads to a desired result. Language is particularly powerful in this way. Taking the above example a bit farther, I could also ask you to imagine a blue cow—a task easily enough accomplished for most people, yet blue cows do not exist in nature. Instead, you have combined the symbolic idea of "blueness" with the symbolic idea of "cow," a minor feat of magick in itself.

ELEMENTALS

In any discussion of the elements, we must also introduce the idea of elementals. These are creatures, or, more accurately, spiritual forms, that underlie the four elements and animate them. We usually choose not to see elementals, but they dance their joy and do their work every moment of every day, all around us.

Elementals are creatures entirely of the element to which they belong. They move and manipulate their element with ease and expertise. Thus, for acts of practical elemental magick, nature magick, or acts of devotion to nature, elementals are often contacted by magicians for assistance, inspiration, and expertise.

Why would an elemental want to help magicians? In my experience, I have found two reasons why they not only help us, but often enjoy doing so. First, elementals are creatures that most people choose not to see in their daily lives. Elementals do enjoy the attention of being noticed, however, though it tends to come as somewhat of a surprise to them when they first notice you noticing them. Second, elementals are normally limited to experiences with their own elements. While one elemental may have interactions with other elements in the complex dance of nature, these do not, for example, give the fire elemental an experience and understanding of water, just because they once made steam together.[5] Their experiences with us, however, allow them to interact with a being that has integrated the four elements and that has a deep understanding of the other three. Thus, they widen their own knowledge of the universe as a result of their interactions with us.[6]

While I have thus far described elementals as playful animators of our world, it is dangerous to assume that they are all joyous and helpful. Many elementals are, indeed, quite beautiful to behold, and playful in their antics. It is, in fact, quite pleasant and exciting to see the fire elemental within the campfire, or the water elemental swimming in the forest stream. Yet, while the fire elementals are responsible for the campfire and the candle flame, they are also responsible for forest fires, flamethrowers, and explosions of dynamite. Air elementals are the light and airy beings moving the summer breeze on your face, but they also drive hurricanes and tornados.[7] Angry elementals, working together, are a truly awesome thing to behold, as any witness to a fairie rade can attest. Their power is no less than the enormous power of nature itself.

Paracelsus held that large natural events were the result of wars fought between different elementals, the resulting cataclysmic display arising from the two dissimilar natures meeting. For example, storms are thought to be wars between water and air; volcanic eruptions are wars between earth and fire; earthquakes result from wars between earth and air. While our culture no longer desires a magical explanation of these events, looking at nature in this way gives us an insight into the energetic nature of the elemental realms.

Elementals are four in type: sylphs (air), gnomes (earth), salamanders (fire), and ondines (water).

WORKING WITH ELEMENTALS

Later we will study the rites that incorporate elementals, but, for now, the focus of the first year or so of study must be on simply discovering the elements within us and learning to see elementals in their native state. It is dangerous to work with any entity before gaining some experience of it as an observer. Elementals can be especially capricious and mischievous to the unprepared and the underprepared.

Air

Astrological Sign:	Gemini, Libra Aquarius
Direction:	East
Elemental:	Sylph
Gender:	Male
Colors:	Yellow, Violet
Elemental Tool:	Dagger
Season:	Spring
Time of Day:	Dawn

From the East, the place of Morning Light, cometh the rushing of the wind wherein the Spirits of Air do dwell...[8]

Travel with me for a few moments and place your imagination on the winds of air. You are the great eagle who takes flight upon the winds to sweep, light and floating, on currents of rising air above a vast forest. You are the hawk who launches herself into flight over empty canyons of air below, circling in the gentle currents of desert air. You are the wind, filling the sails of a great ship at sea, driving it over water, from home to a far land. As you speed over the ocean, it leaps up playfully to share this dance of life with you. You are the Shamal winds, sweeping down from the north across Arabian sand dunes, catching up swirling sands that spin in their circular dances behind you. Some men are thus driven to brilliant thoughts or visions of God in your passing, while others are driven to murder and madness.

Such are the ways of airy nature; they speak loudly about air in all of its forms. Beyond the natures of movement and dance that are the province of air, this element is profoundly important to each and every one of us. For air is also our intellectual clarity and strengths, our ability to discern between two opposing ideas, our ability to think and calculate. Air is associated with the Dagger for many reasons, important among them its hardened, bright steel and its razor edges. These are the attributes of intellect that the magician must develop: the strength of steel, the brilliance of bright metal, the razor edge of discernment.

East

In the Chinese classic, the *Nei Ching*, it is written: "Beginning and creation come from the East." Several times each day, the followers of Islam kneel to the east, singing praises to Allah. In the Orthodox Christian traditions, east is the direction of holy visions, the direction from which God's voice is heard. Magicians begin each day and each rite facing east.

Each day, night is banished, as the Sun rises in the eastern sky. Likewise, it is in the east that the spiritual Sun rises each day. East has long been considered a direction of mystery and all things spiritual. It is difficult for Westerners not to feel some sense of this when we think of that which has come to us from the East: prophets, religions of mystery, yoga, Chinese philosophies, spices, precious stones, and much more. Far East, Middle East, back east are all phrases we use to acknowledge the perceived greater wisdom, depth, and culture of this direction.

Each of us, as we perform the Solar Adoration, cannot help but feel the rising energies of light and warmth as the Sun rises each morning to our joyous call.

Sylphs

The elementals of air are sylphs—also called riders of the night, air spirits, windborn, storm angels, air devas, mindborn, and countless other names associated with winds and the movement of air. This group of elementals includes fairies, banshees, and all winged elementals. Sylphs tend to appear in somewhat human form, and are usually said to be mirthful, eccentric, inconsistent, diligent, and constantly busy.

Table 2 gives some common correspondences for the element of air (see page 134). While this table may serve as a starting point, it is important to begin compiling your own lists of correspondences. You can compile these from books like this one, but it is far more important to begin compiling correspondences from your own experiences. Set aside some sequence of days. On the morning of each day, meditate and visualize the qualities and movements of air. Then, throughout your usual day, record these events, people, objects, and emotions that strike you as being in accord with your airy visions. Over time, this process will lead to a sure knowledge of the element of air in every facet of your life. This knowledge can be of enormous value when you venture into realms above, below, and within this one.

Table 2. Correspondences of Air.*

PSYCHOLOGY	PLANTS	MINERALS	ANIMALS
Diligence (+)	Acacia	Agate	Cardinal
Discrimination	Benzoin	Amethyst	Crow
Flexibilty (+)	Comfrey	Aventurine	Deer
Independence	Elder	Azurite	Dove
Joy (+)	Eucalyptus	Calcite	Eagle
Optimism (+)	Gardenia	Cats Eye	Hawk
Penetration (+)	Honeysuckle	Citrine	Magpie
Wonder (+)	Jasmine	Emerald	Owl
Music (+)	Lavender	Flourite	Peacock
Contempt (-)	Lemon	Jade	Raccoon
Dishonest (-)	Lilac	Jasper	Raven
Frivoloty (-)	Magnolia	Lapis Lazuli	Spider
Gossip (-)	Marjoram	Malachite	Squirrel
Paranoia (-)	Mint	Moonstone	
Sneakiness (-)	Mistletoe	Quartz	
	Nutmeg	Topaz	
	Rose	Turquoise	
	Sandalwood		
	Vines		
	All incense		

*In the Psychology column, I have indicated qualities with (+) and (-). These are not to be interpreted as good and bad, healthy and unhealthy, or useful and negative. Each psychological quality has its place in the balance of our emotional lives; every so-called weakness is a strength at different times in our lives. These symbols are, instead, indicators of a certain polarity within the element. The qualities marked with (+) or (-) will be experienced differently and call for different types of magical work.

Fire

Astrological Sign:	Aries, Leo, Sagittarius
Direction:	South
Elemental:	Salamander
Gender:	Male
Colors:	Red, Green
Elemental Tool:	Wand
Season:	Summer
Time of Day:	Midday

From the South, the place of Flashing Flame, cometh the heart of the radiance wherein the Spirits of Fire do dwell...[9]

Journey with me again in imagination to the equatorial regions of Earth, where the Sun shines warmer and more brightly. You are the heat of our local star, as it is felt on the darkened faces of those who live here. Travel now to the volcanic islands of this part of our globe, where liquid fire flows red from mountains, giving off intense heat that destroys and purifies all in its path. Now see the flames of a funeral pyre as fire rises to consume the empty human shell, freeing the elements within to recombine and re-create, while other matter spirals upward, ever upward, on warm swirls of air, reaching out to the very fire of the stars. Sit now, as we end our journey, in front of a simple candle flame, pure and bright, small but moving with endless energy in a dance that happily swirls about the candle wick, one that would joyfully leap to light the fireplace.

> I am poured out like water, and all my bones are out of joint; my heart is like wax, it is melted in the midst of my bowels.[10]

Fire is the purest element of them all. There is good reason why a flame is used as a symbol of the godhead, and why the lamp symbolizes our purest aspirations. It was, after all, from a burning bush that the Hebrew God once spoke. Fire within us is creativity and drive, our inspiration and will behind those things we want most in life. The Wand is the tool of fire, and it has long been considered the primary tool of the magician. This is understandable, as fire is the magical will, the drive of the magician. Its hot, powerful nature is a lure to new magicians, but fire is the most difficult element to control.

As we know from nature, it is very easy for fire to get out of control and to take on a life and mind of its own. The fire nature can inspire us to great acts of creative, vital magick, but, if we are careless, it can become the forest fire of our downfall, even the madness of the pyromaniac. When we seek courage and strength, however, and to increase the activity and power of a work of practical magick, this is the element to which we turn. See Table 3 (page 138) for the correspondences of the element fire.

South

To anyone living in the northern hemisphere or equitorial regions, the connection between fire and south is simply environmental: the Sun is hottest when in southern skies, and the fires of volcanos and deserts lie to the south.

> From the South there comes extreme heat. Heat pro-
> duces fire and fire produces a bitter flavor.... The powers
> of Summer create heat in Heaven and fire upon Earth.
> They create the pulse within the body and heat within
> the organs. Of the colors they create the red color...and
> they give the human voice the ability to express joy.[11]

Much may be observed in a geographical comparison of tradi-tional cultures of the south with those of the north.

Salamanders

Salamanders are the slithery creatures within fire. No one may light a candle or a match without the help of salamanders, though most of us choose not to see them.

Salamanders have also been known as fire kings or fire spirits, and have been closely connected with virtually every religion or sacred rite that places a flame upon the altar. This group of ele-mentals includes all fire spirits and the devas of India. They are dangerous to humans, yet, when understood and properly approached, they are powerful allies of creation and defense. They appear in many forms, often as slender serpentlike creatures within flames, but they also may be quite large and entirely other than human or animal. Most salamanders are difficult to see, just as any particular flame is difficult to see as it moves. They usually move too quickly for the human eye. Thus, we usually see sala-manders out of the corners of our eyes, often doubting what we have just seen.

Table 3. Correspondences of Fire.

PSYCHOLOGY	PLANTS	MINERALS	ANIMALS
Courage (+)	Allspice	All red stones	Badger
Creativity (+)	Basil	All orange stones	Bear
Idealism (+)	Bay Laurel	Red Agate	Cat
Loyalty (+)	Carnation	Amber	Centaur
Power (+)	Cinnamon	Bloodstone	Coyote
Spirituality (+)	Clove	Carnelian	Fox
Strength (+)	Coriander	Diamond	Hawk
Passion (+)	Garlic	Fire Opal	Lion
Anger (-)	Heliotrope	Garnet	Mouse
Destruction (-)	Holly	Hematite	Porcupine
Impatience (-)	Hyssop	Iron	Ram
Jealousy (-)	Juniper	Red Jasper	Serpent
Vindictiveness(-)	Lavender	Lava	Wolf
	Marigold	Ruby	
	Oak	Sulfur	
	Pepper	Steel	
	Rosemary	Tiger's Eye	
	Rue	Pink Tourmaline	
	Saffron		

Water

Astrological Sign:	Cancer, Pisces, Scorpio
Direction:	West
Elemental:	Ondine
Gender:	Female
Colors:	Blue, Orange
Elemental Tool:	Cup
Season:	Autumn
Time of Day:	Sunset

From the West, the place of Twilight, cometh the sound of the moving waters wherein the Spirits of Water do dwell...[12]

In imagination, sail upon the broad and peaceful oceans, heavy and dense, yet always in fluid motion. Beneath the surface, in cool darkness, seaweeds gently stream out upon deep currents of moving water. You are the dolphin, swimming, diving, and playing in fluid movements of your hydrodynamic form, pushing through your watery world with powerful strokes of your tail. Now, travel to a mountain lake, deep and cold, filled from running streams carrying water from melting snows above. The lake is cool and still, yet in this stillness is a powerful undercurrent of potential movement. The lake is content to sit where it is, but, loosed from its confines, it would joyously tumble down the mountain, fluidly transforming from lake to river. Now you are a rainstorm, driven to the Earth from great height, your fall punctuated by bright lightning and loud thunder. As each of your drops strikes the ground, you are absorbed into it, nourishing living things, pooling in hollows, streaming through beds of stone to join larger streams—always fluid, molding effortlessly to every shape, yet determined in passing. Waters such as these carve rock and sweep away entire cities of humankind.

Water is a lovely element, and one that most magicians seem unsure about how to use. This is the nature of water—fluid, subtle, difficult to pin down. Water is our emotional selves, our fluid, fleeting feelings and dreams. Water is essential to life. It has its own rhythm and cycles. It can be violent or serene, dominating or submissive. It may be frozen as ice, heated into steam, or remain fluid, but it is always water. Water archetypes abound in our culture: the sea journey, the fountain of youth, the magick well, the old watering hole, the rain of tears, the deep blue sea.

The human body is roughly 80 percent water. Within us lie reservoirs, ponds, rivers, seas, currents—the flow of blood, the fluid movements of the lymphatic system. We have within us perspiration, saliva, tears, urine, and sexual fluids. Elemental water makes up our own internal tides and is crucial to our physical and emotional health. Emotionally, water is our own fluidity, our ability to adapt, receive, and feel compassion. Magically, water is the Cup, the quality of receptiveness, devotion, and emotion in ritual. We may turn to water in a rite to help us process an emotional state, or to bring greater fluidity and peace to a troubled, firey life. See Table 4 (page 142) for the correspondences of the element water.

West

West is the direction of broad oceans of water, the direction of the Promised Land, the direction to which early Europeans looked for hope. To the west is the setting Sun, the last glow of orange light over blue seas as day gives way to night. As we practice the Solar Adorations each day, this time begins to take on special meaning. Many have noticed a special peace and quiet associated with sundown and early twilight. East is birth; west is a kind of death, as the Sun willingly gives up its place in the heavens to night, assured of return the next dawn.[13] The cycle of the birth, death, and rebirth of light each day is our microcosmic experience of the larger cycles of the year.

Ondines

This group of elementals is broad. It includes nymphs, mermaids, sirens, harpies, seadaughters, naiads, and many lesser ancient sea gods.[14] All elemental creatures who have their homes in water—ocean, stream, lake, or river—are ondines. Ondines are nearly always beautiful, and beauty is the keynote of their realm. They happily cooperate with humans, usually in the spirit of love and sincerity.

Ondines appear in myriad forms, but most often as seamaidens and other anthropomorphic sea or lake beings. In running water, ondines will often appear as globules of water essence, in balls or in donut shape, or occasionally as sleek, slender eel-like forms. It is said that the voices of ondines may be heard upon warm western winds near evening. Sailors have seen them clinging to the bows of ships (hence the custom of carving women on the bows of ancient ships) and have often heard their beautiful songs.

Table 4. Correspondences of Water.

PSYCHOLOGY	PLANTS	MINERALS	ANIMALS
Compassion (+)	Apple	Agate	Crab
Conscience (+)	Apricot	Amethyst	Dolphin
Devotion (+)	Camphor	Aquamarine	All fish
Forgiveness (+)	Catnip	Azurite	Heron
Receptivity (+)	Chamomile	Celestite	Horse
Tranquility (+)	Cherry	Coral	Jaguar
Dreams (+)	Cyclamen	Stones with holes	Raven
Apathy (-)	Eucalyptus	Jade	Scorpion
Depression (-)	Gardenia	Lapis Lazuli	All shellfish
Frigidity (-)	Hawthorn	Moonstone	
Indifference (-)	Ivy	Pearl	
Insolence (-)	Lotus	Sapphire	
Instability (-)	Melons	Silver	
	Mint	Sodalite	
	Myrrh	Sugalite	
	Narciccus	Tourmaline	
	Orris Root		
	Periwinkle		
	Rose		
	Willow		

Earth

Astrological Sign:	Taurus, Virgo, Capricorn
Direction:	North
Elemental:	Gnome
Gender:	Female
Colors:	Indigo, Gold
Elemental Tool:	Pentacle
Season:	Winter
Time of Day:	Night

From the North, the place of Fertile Earth, cometh the strength of the mountain wherein the Spirits of Earth do dwell...[15]

For our last journey, travel with me once again in imagination as you visit a forest—ancient, dark, and dense. Beneath the trees, the rich soil teams with life, yet is utterly still, infinitely patient and still. With great age comes great perspective. As you dive into the Earth, look back to the forest, to ancient trees that are mere children compared to the rocks and ground to which they cling. Deep within the Earth, feel the pulsing magnetic currents, see the roots seeking nourishment and the seeds springing to new life. You are an enormous stone that has sat in place for thousands of years, moving, but only in geologic terms, your movement invisible to the human eye. You are the stones of Stonehenge, holy relics of an ancient time when humans worked in partnership with stone and earth to honor the divine.

Earth is the ground beneath us. The food we eat is grown in earth and is part of it. The Earth nourishes us and supports us, and for this she has been called Mother Earth. We are sometimes earthy, a particularly sensual aura of life. At other times, we need grounding, to be balanced and centered and stable among the four elements. Earth is this stability and groundedness. It has a rich, sensual nature that is perhaps best characterized by deep and ancient forests. After death, our bodies are often given to the care of earth.[16]

Earth is our stability, our ability to concentrate, stand firm, and wait things out. Those who do not work regularly with earth are often impatient and lose the ability to study effectively. Earth magick is the magick of crystals, sands, salts, and stones. It is the magick of metals and gems. In rites of practical magick, earth is the element associated with money, prosperity, and material gain. Rites of earth should be in the nature of earth: magnetic. Earth rites are most effective when used to charge talismans that magnetically draw some material object or other goal to you.

Without grounding in earth, many magical operations will be superficial at best in their effects. This is why we begin our studies at Lapis Lazuli with the four elements and a grounding in that which is around us in nature. See Table 5 (page 146) for the correspondences of the element earth.

North

The direction north is crucial to our cultural structure and provides numerous rich archetypes: the North Pole, true north, the North Star. Compasses and maps are oriented to the north. North is the direction of stability, truth, and guidance. Steering by the North Star is the truest way home, sailors used to say, and the words are no less true in magical terminology.

North is also the direction of magical happenings: The Good Witch Glenda from the *Wizard of Oz* was the Witch of the North, and, each December, Santa Claus and his eight tiny reindeer leave their home in the north to distribute magick around the world.

Yet frozen winter also comes from the north—cold winds, cold snow, cold water currents in the sea. Winter comes to the northern hemisphere each year bringing its unique ability to crystalize the atmosphere and leaving beautiful crystal structures. In winter, animals hibernate, going deep within themselves to regroup and conserve until spring. Humans have a natural inclination to be cozy and warm during winter, snuggling indoors under blankets and before warm hearths. Stillness, drawing within, regrouping energies, patiently awaiting spring: all very earthy activities.

Gnomes

Gnomes are another rather general category of elementals. They include hobgoblins, elves, forest men, brownies, leprechauns, dwarfs, and many other types of earthy nature spirits. They are often seen by children and heard by those sleeping in forests and groves. They live in caves, among rocks, around stalactites and stalagmites, and are frequently seen around the stones of old castles and other stone structures.

Gnomes are quite amenable to working with humans, but they are limited in scope to the practical, hardworking, earthy activities that suit their nature. For rites of practical, earthy magick, gnomes are useful allies and utterly reliable.

Table 5. Correspondences of Earth.

PSYCHOLOGY	PLANTS	MINERALS	ANIMALS
Concentration (+)	Bayberry	Agate	Ass
Endurance (+)	Berries	Aventurine	Buffalo
Firmness (+)	Cedar	Cat's Eye	Bull
Industry (+)	Cypress	Coal	Cow
Responsibility (+)	Ferns	Emerald	Deer
Self-assurance (+)	Gums	Jasper	Dog
Thoroughness (+)	Honeysuckle	Jet	Dragon
Dullness (-)	Horehound	Malachite	Goat
Unreliability (-)	Jasmine	Marble	Jackal
Laziness (-)	Mosses	Obsidian	Satyr
Misanthropy (-)	Musks	Olivine	Serpent
Tardiness (-)	Myrrh	Onyx	Stag
Uncleanliness (-)	Patchouli	Quartz	Wolf
	Pine	Salt	
	Sage	Sand	
	Violet	Turquoise	

THE FIFTH ELEMENT: SPIRIT

Figure 6. Pentagram.

While the world around us may be seen as made up of four elemental ideas, there is still something that runs beneath and above the physical realm: spirit. You will explore much more of this idea of spirit in your own practices, and you already have a grasp of it from your lighting of the lamp and the Calyx. It is mentioned as a fifth element here primarily because the pentagram, that powerful symbol of the manifest world, has five points (see figure 6, page 146). Each point is attributed to one of the elements. The top point is attributed to spirit. The upward orientation of the spirit symbolizes its ability to transcend nature. When the spirit points downward, it symbolizes spirit descending into nature.[17]

The pentagram enters Aurum Solis practice with the Setting of the Wards. In this rite, another Warding rite like the Circle of Light, the pentagram is visualized. The elemental attributions of the pentagram are not taken into account in this context, as the symbol is to be considered a balance of all the forces encompassed by the points.

The Setting of the Wards of Power

1. Stand in the center of the place of working, or as near the center as the arrangement of the chamber will allow. If the Bomos is situated at the center, begin east of the Bomos.
2. Facing east, perform the Calyx.
3. Advance to the east. Beginning at that point and returning thereto, move counterclockwise around the place of working with your hand outstretched, tracing the circle. After completing the circle, return to center and face east.
    Vibrate: Η' ΠΕΛΕΙΑ ΚΑΙ Η ΥΓΡΑ (HE PELEIA KAI HE HUGRA)
    Ο ΟΦΙΣ ΚΑΙ ΤΟ ΩΙΟΝ (HO OPHIS KAI TO OION)

4. While still facing east, make the gesture *Cervus*

   Vibrate at 1st point: ΑΘΑΝΑΤΟΣ **(ATHANATOS)**

   Vibrate at 2nd point: ΣΕΛΑΗ ΓΕΝΕΤΗΣ **(SELAE-GENETES)**

5. Turn to face north: make the gesture *Cervus*

   1st point: ΙΣΧΨΡΟΣ **(ISCHYROS)**

   2nd point: ΚΥΡΙΟΣ **(KYRIOS)**

6. Face west: make the gesture *Cervus*

   1st point: ΙΣΧΨΡΟΣ **(ISCHYROS)**

   2nd point: ΠΑΝΚΡΑΤΗΣ **(PANKRATES)**

7. Face south: make the gesture *Cervus*

   1st point: ΑΘΑΝΑΤΟΣ **(ATHANATOS)**

   2nd point: ΘΕΟΣ **(THEOS)**

8. Face east. Assume the Wand posture.

   Vibrate: ΓΑΙΑ ΚΑΙ Ο ΙΧΩΡ ΤΟΥ ΟΥΡΑΝΟΥ **(GAIA KAI HO ICHOR TOU OURANOU)**

9. Still facing east, raise your arms to a Tau (see The Calyx, page 100).

   Vibrate:

TO THE EAST ΣΟΤΗΡ	**(SOTER)**
TO THE SOUTH ΑΛΑΣΤΩΡ	**(ALASTOR)**
TO THE WEST ΑΣΦΑΛΕΙΟΣ	**(ASPHALEIOS)**
TO THE NORTH ΑΜΥΝΤΩΡ	**(AMYNTOR)**

10. Repeat the Calyx.

Notes for the Wards of Power

1. After the Calyx, advance to the east. Moving counterclockwise around the place of working your outstretched right hand traces the circle. Visualize a shimmering wall of silver mist that is drawn around the place of working by your out-

stretched hand, until by returning to the east, you have completed the circle and drawn closed the curtain.

2. Return to the center. Facing east, vibrate **HE PELEIA KAI HE HUGRA, HO OPHIS KAI TO OIN,** which in English means "the Dove and the Waters, the Serpent and the Egg."

3. Still facing east, assume the first Cervus position (see figure 7). At the first point, visualize a pentagram of brilliant light on your forehead, framed by your hands.

Figure 7. First Cervus position.

4. Hold this visualization in your thoughts and vibrate
    ATHANATOS. To assume the second Cervus position (see
    figure 8), thrust the pentagram east, forward and
    away from you while you vibrate **SELAE-GENETES.**

Figure 8. Second Cervus position.

5. As the pentagram comes into contact with the mist curtain, visualize it diffusing into the mist in a burst of light. The result of this action is twofold: the forces of air are banished from the circle, and the first Ward is established.

6. Repeat this process for the other three Wards, turning in place, using the directions and divine names shown in the rite. When you have finished setting the Wards, turn again to face east.

7. Assume the Wand posture and vibrate **AIA KAI HO ICHOR TOU OURANOU** (Earth and the Blood of Heaven). Raise your arms to a Tau (see The Calyx, page 100). Your arms will remain in this posture throughout the following invocation.

8. Before you, visualize a tall and slender form, clad in a voluminous and billowing robe of yellow, highlighted with traces of violet. While you contemplate this figure, feel a cool rushing of wind, coming from the east. This wind should be felt inwardly to awaken the hidden aspirations and wordless hopes that have lain dormant in the toils of sloth and habitude: it sings to your inner ear of the potentialities of a life that reaches forth to the spiritual heights. When this image has been formulated and realized, vibrate: **To the East, SOTER** (also called RAPHAEL in other traditions).

9. To the south, visualize a lean muscular figure with an appearance of great strength standing amid flames, clad in a robe of brilliant red with changing sparks of green. This figure holds in the right hand a wand of burnished copper. While you contemplate this figure, feel a sensation of powerful heat coming from the south. Inwardly, you should realize that this heat is generated by the fire of inspiration: there is in its power a kernel of inebriation, as well, as may

be understood by recalling that Dionysus was born from the all-consuming fire of Zeus. When this image has been formulated and realized, vibrate: **To the South, ALASTOR** (also called MICHAEL in other traditions).

10. To the west, visualize a tall and powerful figure standing amid foaming and turbulent waters, clad in a robe of blue with highlights of orange, holding in its left hand a silver cup. While you contemplate this figure, imagine the mighty surge of the sea tides pouring in successive waves from the west. Inwardly, these waves are the cold and shining waters that purify the intellect in their flood, healing it of unreason's fever and tempering it as steel is tempered. When this image has been formulated and realized, vibrate: **To the West, ASPHALEIOS** (also called GABRIEL in other traditions).

11. To the North, visualize a broad-shouldered, placid figure, robed in indigo that gleams with flashes of pale gold, and standing upon wild grass studded with yellow flowers. In its left hand the figure bears a golden orb; in its right a golden sickle. While you contemplate this figure, imagine a feeling of great peace and stability, for the succession of the seasons wipes out or mitigates past errors: the innocence of the Golden Age ever awaits us in the Earth's renewal. Elemental earth itself is the medium of nature's work (and nature, it is to be remembered, is God made manifest). The instinctual faculties of man find their repose within. When this image has been formulated and realized, vibrate: **To the North, AMYNTOR** (also called AURIEL in other traditions).

12. Still in the center of the circle and facing east, lower your arms to a Wand posture. Take a breath or two, then conclude the ritual with a repetition of the Calyx.

Further Notes on the Wards

The visualization of the archangels should be as complete as possible, its details filled in as fully as possible. I once found an excellent fictional description of an experience with an archangel that is just one example of how the symbolism associated with this quarter may be developed in visualizations:

> The space beyond was all pale light and moving air. As [the adept] guided [the student] forward, leaving the others behind, the light and air took the visual form of diaphanous golden curtains billowing in a shimmering breeze. As they passed through the curtains, a fragrance like a breath of frankincense hung on the air. Beyond lay a vast, airy hall flooded with pale golden light and, in its center, a tall pillar of golden light which slowly resolved before [the student's] dazzled eyes into a guazy image vaguely human in form, with a suggestion of sweeping wings that filled all the hall with the vital winds of their beating.
>
> Eyes that were like deep lakes of living gold bent down upon him from a face neither male nor female but supremely beautiful in its androgynous delicacy. Points of golden fire were twined like a diadem through the floating tresses of golden hair flowing back from a high, noble brow.[18]

While your own experience of the archangel of the east will almost certainly differ from this one, merely seeing angels in each quarter with few if any distinguishing characteristics is not sufficient. These archangels should, upon full visualization, strike you as dissimilar to one another as if you were circled by four people of vastly different cultures and languages.

You may notice, in performing the fourfold invocation, that the archangels seem to have gender. In reality, archangels are genderless, but the directions they represent in this ritual do have genderlike qualities or polarities. The usual arrangement is for the east and south to have a male polarity, and the west and north to have a female polarity. At this point, this is not an important distinction and is subject to change, depending on what you are trying to accomplish. I encourage you, however, not to become too attached to the gender of one archangel or another, since this only limits what they really are.

THE MAGICAL VOICE AND RITUAL MOVEMENTS

Now that you have a more complete rite in hand, it is time to work on the movements and vocals. It is important, in a ritual, that your movements be done with great precision—hand position, finger position, head angles, body positioning, foot placement. Sloppy rituals bring sloppy results, and, as magick is one method for learning control of self, it is important to extend that control to your movements. For all of this precision of movement, however, it is also important that ritual movements flow from one to the next. Each ritual is a dance, a concept that will grow in importance as you progress through the system. Dance your invocations, dance your circles, dance with purpose, dance with joy, but dance! As to vocals, it is also important to begin work on making your utterances dramatic. Ritual, while a dance, is also high drama, a bit of playacting for the soul. Speak your lines with feeling, slowly, with emotion behind them, as you would if you were acting the part of a royal and powerful personage talking to the gods as an equal.

This part of your ritual development will take time. It may be aided by watching dancers, buying books about dance, even taking dance lessons. Your vocals may be developed by studying materials about acting: books, cassette tapes, videos, watching movies with high-quality dramatic acting. Shakespeare is an excellent choice, and Kenneth Branaugh's movies have much to recommend them for their use of language and speech.

Finally, take care in performing the Setting of the Wards. It is the fundamental ritual upon which all others are built, and the success of every other ritual depends upon it. Moreover, it will become the foundation of your astral defense. In learning and performing it, always remember the lesson of Achilles: one small hole in your armor is all it takes for your Wards to be defeated, either preventing your consecration of a space for work or exposing you to forces you do not want to face apart from your Wards.

When the integration of gestures, vibrations, visualizations and other parts of the Setting has been achieved, the student should accustom himself to performing the Setting of the Wards, and to working within their protection. To this end, he should carry out the Setting very often, and always before his exercise sequence or any other magical work.

One of the effects of the practice is a personal attunement to the equilibrium of the great forces invoked therein. Long familiarity with this ritual will but render it more rewarding; care must be taken, however, that it is always performed attentively and with unabated heed to all its parts.

The circle traced about the place of working should encompass the whole area, all necessary equipment having been duly placed beforehand within its limits. This is of vital importance, as no-one is to cross the bounds of the circle during the working. No relaxation of this rule should be permitted. If the circle is disturbed in this way, there is a real danger that undesirable influences attracted by the magick may enter through the breach and vitiate the working. A more insidious danger, however, is that the operator who is careless concerning the breaking of his defences will find that he has weakened his own belief in their reality; and such doubts carry their own perils. One's work must be sound, and one must know it to be sound.[19]

STUDY REVISITED

Magick is not primarily an intellectual enterprise. For all the correspondences of magick, the rites, the symbols, the tools mean little if one loses contact with life.

When the original *Magical Philosophy* series came into print, it was common for solitary practitioners to give scant attention to all but the last book, *Mysteria Magica,* where they believed the essence of the Order to reside. This thick text of rites and correspondences, however, was not the essence of Aurum Solis. It was the other texts that showed the student how to integrate the experiences of these rites back into their lives and their psyches, and how to use their lives and psyches in the performance of the rites, weaving Life back into to the tabulated lists and ritual directions. All must be performed for the greater goal of regeneration and the discovery of the true self.

Throughout our study of Art Magick, it is vitally[20] important never to separate the learning of magick from the learning of life. Far too often, I have seen magicians retreat into progressively smaller and smaller worlds, all the while believing they are growing. As Marsilio Ficino advised his students and friends:

> If you compress water into a sponge and squeeze it, you immediately lose it. If you give it more room you will retain it, and this goes even more for air, fire and aether.
>
> These are discussed in vain by the Poets, who struggle to grab the images of Gods and spirits by the elbows. They must be received instead in the widest possible way. Liquid, and extremely abundant, they must be possessed abundantly.
>
> Those who ponder heavily on their studies and business and always work very exactly on tiny matters wear out their lives, or miserably waste away their lives in private. Pythagoras seems to have been right, therefore, in what he taught: Beware, lest you get boxed into some narrow space where there is no more sky for you and nothing more that is vital.[21]

11

QABALAH

The Qabalah, a word meaning "reception" and "tradition," is not a book, but a way of thought. It has impacted the Western world in a fundamental way. Indeed, it is difficult to find a book or teacher of philosophy, ethics, religion, psychology, or magick that does not use this system of thought to some degree, often unaware. Qabalistic thinking underpins almost every major Western religion, from Judaism to Christianity, and the study has fascinated Eastern thinkers for generations.

The value of the Qabalah to the study of magick is that its powerful symbols give us keys to a deep understanding of ourselves and a map of the structure of the universe that can guide us. All that may be known by man is encompassed in this tradition, from the grossest understandings of matter to the highest and most refined, unreachable aspirations of the human heart.

Go to the bookstore and ask to see books on Qabalah and you will quickly notice that there are essentially three related traditions of Qabalistic thought: the philosophical Qabalah, those who study the system as a philosophy with application to psychology and other practical uses; the religious Qabalah, used by serious seekers of the divine, mostly Jewish, to understand God's word to us, to amplify spiritual traditions, and to come closer to knowing God; and the magical Qabalah, used by magicians as a key to the universe, a gateway through which we may step into other realms and move closer to the light. It is this last tradition to which we apply ourselves in the study of Art Magick.

Earlier in this book, you did work toward understanding the idea of archetypes and how they may be used to see patterns in your own life and your magical studies. In your study of the divine archetypes of the Qabalah, all that previous work will now blossom to fruition.[1]

Before I begin to summarize some of the major ideas of the Qabalah, let me warn you that this chapter is not a study or exploration of Qabalistic thought to any great depth. The Qabalah is an enormous field of study, and there is little I can write here that has not already been written. In the Recommended Additional Reading section you will find references to books that provide good starting points toward understanding the magical Qabalah. Don't worry about buying a lot of them all at once, for this may not yield the benefits you may think. This time-honored divine tradition is a course of study that cannot possibly be encompassed in one lifetime, and probably not even in two or three.

To buy many books on Qabalah and read them all is rather like using a coffee cup to bail the ocean: it really doesn't matter how fast you go, you will not be finished anytime soon and you'll miss some wonderful sunsets in the process.[2] The Qabalah is a way of thought, not a course of study. It is far more important to draw the basic concepts of Qabalah within you, deeply and irrevocably, than it is to read what one author after another has said on the subject. There is nothing more un-Qabalistic than to hear two magicians argue about the differing views of two *other* magicians on some fine point of a sephiroth or a path. As with any map, whether of this world or beyond, it is the journey that matters, not the pale and inadequate shadow of the journey that may be captured on paper.

THE FOUR WORLDS

One fundamental idea of Qabalah is the model of the four worlds. The oldest known example of this concept is a 12th-century text, *Masekheth Atsiluth*, that translates as the *Treatise on Emanation*. This book, like many other books on Qabalah, explores the Tree of Life and other ideas, but adds a simple presentation of the four worlds, integrating them with other Qabalistic concepts. While this is the root text from which much of our current understanding of the four worlds is drawn, the concept is an ancient one, perhaps even older than the emanations and Tree of Life model. It has been meticulously developed by Qabalists to become a central support structure of Qabalism.

Simply stated, the four worlds are planes, realms, or worlds that act to veil us from the divine, and through which the divine is manifested on Earth. In one sense, all four worlds exist in parallel and simultaneously. Thus, each world may be used to describe a particular quality or aspect of every action and object in our universe. The primary characteristics of the four worlds are summarized in Table 6 (page 162).

Nothing exists purely in one world or another; everything has reflection and expression in all four worlds.

For example, I may look at a tree outside my window. Clearly,

Table 6. Characteristics of the Four Worlds.

WORLD	CHARACTERISTIC
Atziluth	World of Emanation, Divine Archetypes, Sephiroth and Planets in purest form.
Briah	World of Creation, World of Intellect, Archangels, Gods and Goddesses.
Yetzirah	World of Formation, Astral Light, World of Emotion, Shifting Images.
Assiah	World of Manifestation, Physical Universe, Nature, Human Existence.

the tree exists in this moment of time in the world of manifestation, Assiah, but it also has an astral reflection in the world of formation, Yetzirah. Beyond this, I know that the tree has come into creation and is continually recreated from the original idea of tree, taking the potential for shape in the world of creation, Briah. Finally, this creation can only follow the patterns of true and divine archetypes of all-that-is, and these are found in the world of emanation, Atziluth. Each of these aspects of the tree I view in any instant of time and space.

In another sense, these worlds exist in a sort of hierarchy, from which the root archetypes of all the cosmos light the spark of manifestation and filter through the four worlds to reach the manifested state we see around us. The light that begins in one world is more grossly expressed in each succeeding world, until it finds form.[3]

Viewed in this way, the tree outside my window encompasses process of manifestation from that-which-was-not into that-which-is. I follow with fascination the development of the tree from divine archetype to manifestation in all of its green strength and grace. In my thoughts, this takes place as a process of descending light, from emanation, to creation, to formation, to manifestation, as if these happen one after the other.

Finally, the four worlds, when viewed from our perspective here on Earth, become a series of veils through which we may pass only with work, study, and profound inner change.

The tree outside my window exists in four worlds, and is a product of light descending through the four worlds—these things I know. Yet there is a problem and a mystery in the moment of being faced with the tree and wishing to use it as a vehicle for reaching beyond and into these other realms. To understand the tree in the four worlds intellectually is relatively easy. To use the tree as a gateway through which to traverse the four worlds is a task far beyond academic discussion and intellectual pursuit.

Atziluth

Atziluth is the first world, the world of emanation, in which the divine manifests in the form of abstract archetypes. These root images are the basis for all creation and begin the first cause of manifestation from which all existence springs. This is also the world in which the sephiroth of the Tree of Life first manifest themselves, where they reside in their highest and most pure forms. Nothing in this world or any other is static, and it must be remembered at all times that manifestation is a moment-by-moment process of creation and re-creation, endless and eternal. The same is true of Atziluth, where divine archetypes reside, but are continually created and re-creating, manifested in a fluid, continuous raying-out of the inexhaustable energy of the hidden divine One in the form of pure ideas that become models for all-that-is. The seven traditional planetary archetypes begin here as well, though they exist here only as ideals or principles of archetypical significance (see Table 7).

Table 7. Planetary Energies.

PLANET	ENERGY
Saturn	Changeless Stability
Jupiter	Majestic Beneficence
Mars	Valiant Strength
Sun	Lifegiving Splendor
Venus	Celestial Love
Mercury	Spirit of Wisdom
Moon	Change and Becoming

Briah

Briah is the world of creation where, as the lights of the sephiroth stream forth from Atziluth, the Merkabah (divine throne-chariot or heavenly hall of thrones) takes form. Herein resides the archangels and all the great gods and goddesses to whom humans have prayed. It is written in Qabalistic literature that, when the unformed light of emanation penetrates this world, these angels and gods joyously gather around to lend it shape, forming the body of manifestation.

Briah is also known as the world of intellect, the world of pure ideas and thoughts, devoid of influence by emotion or aspiration. These are the pure ideas that bring a primitive shamanistic system into maturity, as a theology is developed and philosophies are considered, through which an increasing number of spiritual values are discovered, discerned, or imagined.[4] It is at this time that what begins as a simple relationship between a god or goddess, which exists primarily on the astral plane, becomes a channel of force between the worshippers and the world of Briah. From this, their conception of goddess or god is given increasing life from the world of divine creation, establishing the deity. As long as a people continue to worship this deity, the form remains active and the channel remains open. Eventually, if the deity is long ignored, the archetypal force is withdrawn and the link to the world of Briah is lost.

> Thereafter anyone desiring to invoke the deity will have to work arduously from basic principles to establish what will in fact be a new cult. This may not succeed, owing to fundamental changes in methods of approach or modes of thought; nevertheless, it is occasionally a matter for awe, to see what living echoes from ancient time can be reawakened by one who has the authentic keys and who has worked patiently to re-establish the link.[5]

Here again, the traditional seven planets have formation, as do the gods and goddesses associated with them. A few examples, by no means comprehensive, are given in Table 8 (see page 166).

Yetzirah

The third world is Yetzirah, the world of formation, also known as the astral plane. "As above, so below," is the ancient

Table 8. Planetary Divinities.

PLANET	DEITY
Saturn	Hera, Kronos, Aphrodite Ourania, Iuno, Saeturnus, Ishtar, Kali, Shiva, Brahma, Net, Ptah
Jupiter	Zeus, Athene, Poseidon, Iuppiter, Minerva, Indra, Sarasvati, Maat, Amun-Ra
Mars	Ares, Hephaistos, Mars, Volcanus, Agni, Durga, Heru-Behutet, Sekhet
Sun	Apollo, Dionysus, Helios, Sol, Vishnu, Ra
Venus	Aphrodite, Venus, Lakshmi, Bast
Mercury	Hermes, Mercurius, Ganesha, Thoth
Moon	Artemis, Selene, Hecate, Diana, Varuna, Shiva, Khonsu

maxim. Yetzirah is the principal place where manifestation takes shape and other characteristics acquired before a primal concept passes the last veil into physical manifestation. Yetzirah may also be thought of as the substance of the world of assiah, in that the astral plane underlies the physical plane, and there is a continual interchange of causality between them. Manifestation and change happen in Yetzirah before they happen in Assiah (in one sense), and in this fact lies the key to much of magick and nearly all of the psychic talents.

Yetzirah is a confusing world of shifting images, not only those descending from Atziluth through Briah, but also many forms generated from Assiah. Most of these latter forms are generated spontaneously from the emotions of humans, but thought may also create them. When this is done deliberately and with planning, we call it practical magick or creative visualization. Images in Yetzirah shift and move continuously, tossed about by emotion that changes and moves them as the wind moves clouds. Focused thought can fix them in place, however, creating a path for manifestation in Assiah.

Aside from these shifting and fluid images and forms, Yetzirah does have its own inhabitants: intelligences and powers of various natures, elementals, and the spirits of the seven planetary spheres.

Assiah

Finally, we come to the world of assiah, the world of manifestation or the world of making. This is the world of matter, of nature, and of human existence. As one Order document states in the modern Qabalistic philosophy of Aurum Solis, Assiah *is* Matter: it is the material manifestation of those forces whose pattern is established on the inner causal planes (Atziluth, Briah, and Yetzirah).

TYING THINGS TOGETHER

The intellectual aspect of the study of magick is not merely the memorization of various tables of symbols and correspondences. The task is to interweave and relate each new set of correspondences with those you have previously learned. These relationships between symbolic sets aid in understanding each set in greater depth, and allow us to quickly chart alternative routes to a single magical destination.

The first valuable correspondences are between our previous

understanding of the four elements and the four worlds. In this relationship, each of the four worlds is associated with one letter of the Tetragrammaton. These, in turn, correspond to the elements. Thus, the world of Atziluth corresponds to fire, the world of Briah corresponds to water, the world of Yetzirah corresponds to air, and the world of Assiah corresponds to earth. Review what you know about each of the elements, and what you have just read about each of these worlds, and you will find that there are areas of overlap, as well as areas of difference. The inspiration you find in one can help you to understand the other. This is the value of correspondences—one set layered upon another, each putting a particular idea in larger and larger context, until the smallest and most insignificant object in your world can be understood in the context of divine manifestation.

Another correspondence may be found between the Hebrew characters of the Tetragrammaton, the divine four-letter name of God, and the four worlds. We first discussed the letters Yod, Heh, Vau, and Heh in chapter 6. Now we will explore the relationship of Taoist thought and Qabalistic creation to this new realm of the four worlds. In this model, Atziluth corresponds to Yod, Briah corresponds to the first Heh, Yetzirah corresponds to Vau, and Assiah corresponds to the final Heh. If you look back to our earlier discussion of these letters, you will discover why some of our discussion of the four worlds may have struck you as familiar. There is simply no way to overestimate the value of the symbolism, nor the value of the symbols as they correspond to one another. These are basic tools of magick and have been the largest and most important parts of the secret magical archives of the great Orders.

THE AIN SOPH

> No matter how much one Kabbalist may differ from
> another in his theoretical speculations he will agree that
> without the concepts of the En-Sof and the Sefiroth,
> there is no Kabbalism. He might even add that with
> these two concepts the whole of Kabbalism may be
> understood without further commentary.[6]

The concept of *Ain Soph*, however, belongs to the realm of mysticism, and is not within the reach of magical training or practice. Yet a concept so crucial to the Qabalist cannot be entirely ignored.

The term Ain Soph means "without limits" or "without end." It is upon the word "without" that our attention should be focused, for this is a concept of nothingness far beyond our comprehension. To describe Ain Soph is beyond human language, but it may be approximated by the idea of negative existence—that is to say, the Ain Soph exists in nonexistence and that nonexistence, it exists. All other attempts to classify or label the Ain Soph will fail, for to do so is to speak of it in existence and, at that point, we have lost it.

Nor can we speak of the Ain Soph in negative terms, such as those of Pseudo-Dionysus:

> The cause of all things is neither soul nor intellect; nor
> has it imagination, opinion, or reason, or intelligence;
> nor is it reason or intelligence; nor is it spoken or
> thought. It is neither number, nor order, nor magnitude,
> nor littleness, nor equality, nor inequality, nor similar-
> ity, nor dissimilarity. It neither stands, nor moves, nor
> rests. It is neither essence, nor eternity, nor time. Even

intellectual contact does not belong to it. It is neither science nor truth. It is not even royalty or wisdom; not one; not unity; not divinity or goodness; nor even spirit as we know it.[7]

Yet such a negation of all things leaves us with nothing, in itself a concept and therefore not the Ain Soph. The Chinese have the same difficulty in expressing this concept, which they call Tao:

The tao that can be spoken
is not the eternal Tao.
The name that can be named
is not the eternal Name...
Free from desire,
you will know the mystery.
Caught in desire,
you will see only the manifestations.[8]

The Ain Soph precedes our concepts of gods and goddesses, as well as our concept of the highest realms of Atziluth. There is no place in space or time in which it exists. It was not the creator of our cosmos, for the desire and act of creation are some-thing and therefore not the Ain Soph. The Ain Soph is before all beginnings, is after all endings.

In Eastern thought, there is a practice, approached through the use of *koans* and other similar patterns of thought and symbol, designed to create a moment of instability and paradox in the mind. Thus, the famous koan, What is the sound of one hand clapping?, creates a paradox in which we try to understand the sound of something that makes no sound. In this moment of paradox, as our mind attempts to wrap itself around an impossible concept, we may approach, if only for a brief moment, the essence of this idea.

This section of this book (or any book) is actually quite useless in understanding the Ain Soph, for, when I began writing, I had already lost it; when you began reading this chapter, you had already lost it. When we saw the word Ain Soph for the first time, we had already lost it. In this text, the Ain Soph would best be represented by a missing page, for which there is no sign of a missing page: the missing page between pages 134 and 135, the page that does not exist, yet that has not even nonexistence, for it was never conceived.

I remember an exercise in seminary in which we were asked to begin a series of meditations toward experiencing moments of transcendant emptiness and nothingness. If, in the beginning, God created the heaven and the Earth, we were asked, where was God before there was a place to be? What came before lightness and darkness? After spending a great deal of effort on these meditations and prayers, we were quite pleased at the moments of "nothingness" we experienced. Yet, as each of us went to the monk who taught the class to report our success, we were told, "Ah, now you have experienced nothingness, yet this is nothing more than the other half of God. Now that you have experienced both what is and what is not, know that between them is something from which both existence and nonexistence sprang forth." It was some time later that I realized he was talking about what the Qabalists call the Ain Soph.

The essence of the concept is all we need to keep in mind in the study of magick. We should also always remember that, as wonderful as we believe our intellects to be, we do, in fact, have numerous limitations of perspective and understanding. There are things (and no-things) in this universe that are simply beyond our ability to comprehend. Our highest, most noble, most refined aspirations toward the divine are merely one small aspect of all-that-is, all-that-is-not, and all-that-is-between those ideas. That is why I call my study and meditations on this concept my "humility exercises."

THE SEPHIROTH

> He made ten lights spring forth from His midst, lights which shine with the form which they have borrowed from Him, and which shed everywhere the light of a brilliant day. The Ancient One, the most Hidden of the hidden, is a high beacon, and we know Him only by His lights, which illuminate our eyes so abundantly. His Holy Name is no other thing than these lights.[9]

These ten lights are thought of as dynamic modes of being, or abstract entities of change, or currents of "beingness." All of these concepts hold within them the twofold nature of the sephiroth. They are modes, currents, or vehicles through which the light descends into manifestation, but they are also root archetypes of what is constant.

The sephiroth are ten in number, with unique names, qualities, symbols, and places in the scheme of the four worlds. There are no more than ten; there are no less. This is important, as the *Sepher Yetsirah* states:

> There are ten Sephiroth. Ten, and not nine; ten, and not eleven. If one acts and attempts to understand this Wisdom, he shall become wise.[10]

Table 9 outlines the essential names and qualities of the sephiroth.

Table 9. The Essential Correspondences of the Sephiroth.

NUMBER	HEBREW	ENGLISH	QUALITY
1	Kether	Crown	Unity
2	Chokmah	Wisdom	Expansion
3	Binah	Understanding	Constriction
4	Chesed	Mercy	Order
5	Geburah	Strength	Energy
6	Tipareth	Beauty	Equilibrium
7	Netzach	Victory	Combination
8	Hod	Splendor	Separation
9	Yesod	Foundation	Conception
10	Malkuth	Kingdom	Realization

THE TREE OF LIFE

The sephiroth have internal relationships and an order of divine emanation. This is usually referred to as a lightning flash of light from the divine mind, flashing from one sephirah to another in an order that achieves balance. The most common method for visually representing this sequence and balance is in a diagram known as the Tree of Life. This is almost certainly familiar to many readers, especially in the form shown in figure 9 (page 174).[11]

The Supernal Triad

The first three sephiroth—Crown, Wisdom, and Under-standing—together form the Supernal Triad and symbolize the three primary aspects of knowledge. It is often said that the

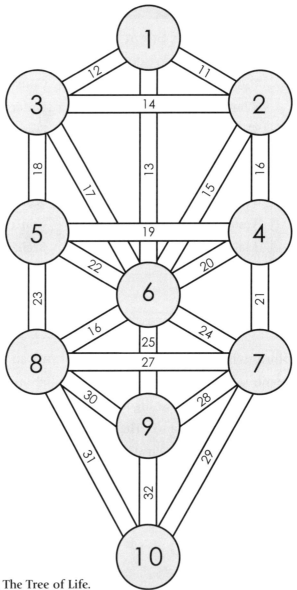

Figure 9. The Tree of Life.

Supernal Triad comprises a level that is not reachable through the operations of magick. This is the realm of mystics, for we may not "act" our way into the Supernals, but only receive them into our understanding, and perhaps even that may not be accomplished while still living on Earth.

Kether

Kether is the first sephirah, the Crown. This is the first state of existence, one of pure light and glory in perfect unity. Within this sephirah, the plan of the entire cosmos is contained, and from here all flows into manifestation.

Kether is also called the Old One, the Primordial Point, the Ancient of Ancients, the Smooth Point, the White Head, the Inscrutable Height, the Vast Countenance, and the Bottomless Fount of All the Ages.

Chokmah

Chokmah is the second sephirah, Wisdom. This is the principle of fatherhood in the divine, where the seeds of all things spiritual, astral, or material are housed. It is the storehouse of first ideas, the *logoi spermatikoi,* which, as seeds, are passed to Binah. While Kether contains the plan of the cosmos as received from the Ain Soph, Chokmah contains the plane with the impetus to create, the burst of desire and impulse of divine will to stream out the plan of creation.

While this sephirah is associated with the concept of divine fatherhood, you may have noticed that it is also associated with wisdom, *Sophia,* usually a feminine concept. Moreover, it is not unusual to hear Qabalists refer to Chokmah as "she" and "her." The apparent contradiction is a contradiction only to those of us who are conditioned to dividing all things into male and female.

The sephirah, however, are androgynous to some degree, and possess functions and characteristics of both genders. As pointed out by some Qabalists, each sephirah has the essential quality of receptive femininity in its relationship to the sephirah that immediately precedes it, and the essential quality of male transmission in relationship to the Sephirah that follows.

Chokmah is also called the Gushing Fountain, Water of the Wise, and the Supernal Father.

Binah

Binah, the third sephirah, is Understanding. This sphere emanates the essential principle of divine motherhood, receptive wisdom, bringing the seeds from Chokmah into formation of everything that will have existence in the realms of light and life.

This sephirah is also known as the Supernal Mother.

Below the Supernal Triad

The sephiroth below the Supernal Triad contain qualities that are more easily understood and explored by us. These include mercy, strength, beauty, victory, and splendor.

Chesed

The fourth sephirah is Chesed—Mercy, or Loving Kindness. It is also called Gedulah, Magnificence. This is the quality of divine mercy and magnanimity, the boundless abundance of the universe. Qabalists hold that this sphere symbolically represents the first day of creation, when God created light and separated light from darkness to make the first day and night.

Geburah

The fifth sephirah is Geburah—Strength, also called Power and Judgment. This is the quality of direction and control of the creative emanation from above. The limitless mercy of Chesed is here restricted and limited, just as Chesed lends tempering to the qualities of Geburah. This is also the principle of divine justice. Mercy and justice are an age-old pairing, for without justice, mercy errs through excess.

Symbolically, this is the second day of creation, when God created a firmament in the midst of the waters. From this, the waters were separated, those above heaven (the firmament) and those below it, introducing a constriction and direction to the outflowing of creation in the first day.

Tiphareth

The sixth sephirah is Tipareth—Beauty. This is the sphere that unites the lines and qualities of creative light from above into a gentler transmission of the outpouring of light from Kether. This sephirah occupies a central place on the Tree of Life, lending an essential androgynous balance to the transmission of forces from above.

It is said that Tiphareth represents the third day of creation, when God created dry land from the waters and commanded the Earth to bring forth grass, the herb yielding seed, and the fruit tree yielding fruit after its kind, whose seed was in itself.

Netzach

The seventh sephirah is Netzach—Victory, an active principle that supports Mercy. Here, the current of light from Tiphareth, shaped by the glory and balance of that sphere, flows forth into the vitality and abundant love of nature. Nature is the essential being of Netzach.

Netzach represents the fourth day of creation, when God made the Sun, the Moon, and the stars, and created the seasons of Earth.

Hod

The eighth sephirah is Hod—Splendor. The essential quality of Hod is to divide and analyze what the divine mind knows as one unity. It is here that the ten thousand things spring into individual existence, and the splendor written of is the bright spark of intellect playing over all of creation. Qabalists hold that Hod symbolizes the fifth day of creation, when fish and birds sprang forth and were commanded to be fruitful and multiply.

Yesod

The ninth sephirah is Yesod—Foundation. Another sephirah holding a central position, Yesod transmits and gives expression to the creative flow from Tiphareth, Netzach, and Hod. The infinitely varied creation from Hod is expressed into the lower worlds here, concentrated and projected upon Malkuth.

Yesod represents the sixth day of creation, when the rest of the animal kingdom sprang forth, and God created Adam and Eve.

Malkuth

Malkuth—the Kingdom—is the tenth sephirah. This is the receptacle of all the lights above, the resolution of the Tree of Life in our world.

Malkuth represents the seventh day of creation, when God rests.

The Ten Sephiroth in the Four Worlds

The ten sephiroth and the four worlds are related concepts in two ways. First, the Tree of Life exists fully in each of the four worlds, each sephirah possessing the qualities above in harmony with the expression of that quality in each world. Think of the four worlds as layers behind each sephirah. For Chesed, for example, there is a divine quality of mercy (Atziluth), an intellectual quality of mercy (Briah), an emotional quality of mercy (Yetzirah), and a physical quality of mercy (Assiah).

Paths on the Tree of Life

You will see on the previous diagram of the Tree of Life that the ten sephiroth are connected by twenty-two numbered paths. The correspondences and working of these paths are beyond the scope of this book, but an outline of essential qualities will serve as an introduction to how the sephiroth communicate their forces between one another. Remember that the paths are not really paths in the sense of something upon which we walk, but are rather states of being, or states of consciousness, encompassing the many modes of mind that lie between us and the divine.

There are some useful correspondences with the paths that can help you to gain a sense of each of these states of consciousness. Three of the most interesting for further independent research and study are the cards of the Major Arcana of the tarot, the influences from planets, elements and the zodiac, and the letters of the Hebrew alphabet. Table 10 summarizes these correspondences (see page 180).

Table 10. Correspondences of the Thirty-two Paths on the Tree of Life.

PATH	CARD	PLANET/ ELEMENT	HEBREW LETTER	HEBREW MEANING
11	The Fool	Air	Aleph	Ox
12	The Magician	Mercury	Beth	House
13	High Priestess	Moon	Gimel	Camel
14	The Empress	Venus	Daleth	Door
15	The Emperor	Aires	Heh	Window
16	The Hierophant	Taurus	Vau	Nail
17	The Lovers	Gemini	Zayin	Sword
18	The Chariot	Cancer	Cheth	Fence
19	Strength	Leo	Teth	Serpent
20	The Hermit	Virgo	Yod	Hand
21	Wheel of Fortune	Jupiter	Kaph	Palm of Hand
22	Justice	Libra	Lamed	Lash
23	The Hanged Man	Water	Mem	Water
24	Death	Scorpio	Nun	Fish
25	Temperance	Sagittarius	Samekh	Support
26	The Devil	Capricorn	Ayin	Eye
27	The Tower	Mars	Peh	Mouth
28	The Star	Aquarius	Tzaddi	Fish-hook
29	The Moon	Pisces	Qoph	Back of Hand
30	The Sun	Sun	Resh	Head
31	Last Judgment	Fire	Shin	Tooth
32	The Universe	Saturn	Tau	Mark

The Ten Sephiroth, the Four Worlds, and the Seven Divine Planets

The seven planets also have attribution to the sephiroth of the Tree of Life (see Table 11). They are corresponded to sephiroth 3 through 10, as it is not until Binah that the whirlings of divine creativity begin to take shape in the sense that planetary archetypes possess.

Table 11. Planets and the Tree of Life.

SEPHIRAH	PLANET
Binah	Saturn
Chesed	Jupiter
Geburah	Mars
Tiphareth	Sun
Netzach	Venus
Hod	Mercury
Yesod	Moon
Malkuth	Earth

USING THE QABALAH

To use the Qabalah, you must develop a sort of Qabalistic mode of thought, feeling, and expression. This requires a familiarity with the Tree of Life and the sephiroth. When you view a painting and like it, the image gives you pleasure for some unknown reason within. This is one mode of thought. The art critic views the painting in comparative terms, measuring the work against standards of art and other artists. Art historians see threads of historical development in the brushstrokes, the canvas, and the colors and techniques used. From this, they can approximate the painting's age and the influences on the artist. Each of these people has come to view the painting as they do because they are familiar with systems and models for the classification of various aspects of the work. They may also simply look at the work and "like it," but their study gives them other interesting tools that provide a specific perspective.

Qabalah is the same sort of tool—a tool for the examination of life and the cosmos. The Qabalist may look at a painting and see the influences of the four worlds, thinking about how art itself and the artistic impulse came to be in the artist. The Qabalist may see colors and patterns in the work that recall a specific sephirah, or are reminiscent of the visual experiences of a particular path. In fact, the painting may possess enough such qualities that the Qabalist purchases it and hangs the work in his or her personal Chamber of Art to serve as inspiration and a focal point while working to achieve a particular pathworking or sphereworking.[12]

This is the time to begin seeing the world around you in Qabalistic terms. Add these correspondences to your own lists and add to them as your own intuition informs. Make copies of a blank Tree of Life (see figure 9, page 174) and practice labeling it with the names of the sephiroth and the numbering of the paths. Once you are familiar with this, begin to layer into your diagrams other correspondences with the Tree. Eventually, pick aspects of the everyday world around you and place them on your Tree of Life. With this essential groundwork in place, the more advanced work of pathworking is open to you.

The Tree Within

As the Tree of Life has correspondences in the world around us, so is it reflected within us as centers of energy. Many spiritual and magical traditions have developed methods for understanding and working with our energetic centers, from the Qi Gong of China to the chakras of India. In the Aurum Solis, students establish a relationship with these important centers through a rite called the Rousing of the Citadels. This rite, to be performed daily by each practitioner of our Art Magick, is a powerful and beneficial technique that will strengthen your magical self. It will add considerable magical energy to each of your rites and, like Qi Gong, benefit your health as well.

The centers of energy touched by this ritual should be visualized as spherical balls of concentrated light and energy, about two to three inches in diameter. There are six of these centers in the Aurum Solis tradition, no more and no less, and each is named: the Corona Flammae is above the head; the Uncia Coeli is upon the brow, half in and half out of the body; the Flos Abysmi is in front of, and external to, the throat; the Orbis Solis is at the middle of the chest, half in and half out of the body; the Cornua Lunae is at the genitals, half in and half out of the body; and the Instita Splendens lies between the insteps of the feet, half above the ground, half below. The Rousing of the Citadels is always preceded with a Warding rite such as the Circle of Light or Wards of Power rites described earlier, and requires proficiency with the Rhythmic Breath technique.

The Rousing of the Citadels

1. Following a Warding rite, face east, and assume the Wand posture.
2. Establish the Rhythmic Breath.
3. Inhale. Visualize the Corona Flammae as a sphere of intense bright white above your head. Visualize the brightness of the light filling and warming the space above you.
4. Exhale, vibrating **EN TO PAN.**
5. Inhale, drawing down a shaft of bright light from the Corona to the Unica Coeli, forming a sphere of bright light upon your forehead. Visualize the light permeating your head, until your head is glowing with warm, healing light.
6. Exhale, vibrating **TURANA.**
7. Inhale, drawing the shaft of light down from the Unica Coeli to the Flos Abysmi, a sphere of bright light outside your body, in front of your throat. Visualize the sphere of light bathing your throat and upper chest with light, feeling your breathing relax. Your lungs and throat move more freely, relaxed but strong.
8. Exhale, vibrating **DESTAPHITON.**
9. Inhale, drawing the shaft of light down from the Flos Abysmi to the Orbis Solis, forming a sphere of bright light at your chest, half in and half out of your body. Visualize the light filling your chest, healing and warming you, giving light to the blood that flows through your heart, light that is distributed through your body by the strong and sure movements of your circulation.
10. Exhale, vibrating **ONOPHIS.**
11. Inhale, drawing the shaft of light down from the Orbis Solis to form the Cornua Lunae, a sphere of bright light at your

groin. Feel the light warm you, awakening this energy center, clearing blockages and flooding your body with health and strength. It is normal to feel sensual, even sexual sensation, as this is a power center connected to the awesome power of creation within us all.

12. Exhale, vibrating **IAO**.

13. Inhale, drawing the shaft of light down from the Cornua Lunae to the Instita Splendens, a sphere of bright light between your feet, half above the ground, half below. Visualize the sphere of light shining upward from the ground, its movements warming your lower body, lazily stirring it like a pool of water.

14. Exhale, vibrating **BATH-MENIN-HEKASTOU.**

15. Inhale, visualizing a thick band of bright white light rising from between your feet, spiraling counterclockwise, moving swiftly upward around your body until it reaches the Flos Abysmi, the sphere in front of your throat, where it is absorbed.

16. Exhale, strengthening your visualization of the Centers and the shaft of light that connects them.

17. Inhale, visualizing a thick band of reddish-white light rising from between your feet, spiraling clockwise, moving swiftly around your body until it, too, is absorbed in the Flos Abysmi.

18. Exhale. Relax, breathing normally, allowing the visualized centers and shaft of light to fade from your conciousness.

This is a large rite, and it will take considerable time and effort to bring the visualizations and the vibrations to proficiency. Do not hurry, for this rite is too important in your magical development to rush through it. After a few weeks, or months, of practice with the rite as shown above, you may begin to add another layer to it: color. Use the table below to add color and movement to your visualizations during the Rousing.

Table 12. Energy Centers and Their Corresponding Colors.

CENTER	COLOR
Corona Flammae	Intense brightness, like burning magnesium.
Uncia Coeli	Dove gray, glimmering.
Flos Abysmi	Purple, intense, and billowing.
Orbis Solis	Yellow, pulsating.
Cornua Lunae	Lavender, radiant and swirling quickly.
Instita Splendens	All seven prismatic colors, swirling lazily.

12

ESTABLISHING A RHYTHM

O ne of the most important aspects of magical work is the establishment of a rhythm of practice. At this point, a number of practices and rites have been introduced and you should have developed a basic daily routine that will serve you throughout your study.

A BASIC DAILY ROUTINE

Below is a basic routine that members of the Lapis Lazuli Commandery are expected to establish within their first year of study. Use this as a check-point for your own daily practice.

- Light the lamp at the beginning of all magical rites;
- Perform a Solar Adoration each morning and evening;
- Wear the robe and ring during rites;
- Practice postures and the rhythmic breath;
- Maintain a magical diary, dream journal, and artisan journal;

- Practice the Calyx daily;
- Practice the Wards of Power or Circle of Light daily;
- Practice mediation daily;
- Contact the four elements.

To accomplish the last item, many members of our Commandery use a combination of spending time in nature for a direct experience of the elements, and this excerpt from an Order document to contact the four elements within:

> It is good for us at some time to keep, for a month or for six months, in addition to the magical record, a diary of our daily thoughts and acts. At the end of the period, we take four pencils: red for Fire, blue for Water, green or brown for Earth, yellow for Air. We go carefully through the written record, judging to the best of our ability the elemental affinities of the matters there written, and we underline the words and phrases in the appropriate colors. So, at the conclusion, we are able to judge whether one or two elements dominate our life, or if one of them is altogether absent, and we can resolve how to establish a better balance. And if Earth be deficient, or Fire, or Water, we should not congratulate ourselves upon our spirituality, but beware of squandering an incarnation.

Of course, another diary can be kept, as suggested, but this technique works quite well in a variety of contexts. The dream journal, letters you have written, e-mail you have sent, poetry or stories you have written: all these are fertile ground for this process of finding the elements within. Familiarity with the technique allows you to apply this analysis to thoughts and feelings on the fly, day by day.[1] Over time, your thoughts may turn to the writings and spoken language of those closest to you, where you will find elemental keys to your relationship to them.

With all such magical self-analysis and analysis of others, however, the goal is not to identify problems or find what's wrong with yourself or another. To find that your employer is strongly embracing fire out of proportion to the rest of the elements while you embrace water is not a diagnosis of either of you. It is, however, a potential key to understanding communications between you and your employer. It is also a key to understanding how you can change your relationship to another person through an awareness of the elements. Magical work to balance the elements within you has some very practical benefits, for the ability to use fire to communicate with fire, and water to communicate with water, for instance, is a powerful one as you move through your world.

Finally, another important concept to look for in this elemental analysis is the fluid, changing nature of yourself and those around you. You may find in your journals and writings that you are predominantly air, or predominantly earth, but you will also see that, season by season, day by day, and hour by hour, you flow through all four elements. Often, this fluid mixing of elements will reveal patterns in your life that help you to find a set of personal correspondences. Integrate your own patterns and thoughts into the other symbolic systems of correspondence given in this and other texts, and you will have made this tool your own.

A WEEKLY RITE: THE WINE BLESSING

Another rite that is simple and quite beautiful is a Wine Blessing rite that many of us use on a weekly basis as a magical Eucharist. There are several forms of this rite used in the Aurum Solis curriculum, including a full ritual of transubstantiation approaching the complexity of the Catholic Tridentine Mass. The simple and short Wine Blessing, however, is much loved and much used at Lapis Lazuli. A simplified form follows.

The Lapis Lazuli Wine Blessing

1. Assume the robe and ring.
2. Place a goblet of wine on the Bomos and light the lamp.
3. Perform the Setting of the Wards or Circle of Light rite.
4. Stand facing east, your Bomos before you. Raise the goblet before you with both hands and dedicate it, saying:

> **To the Powers of Light**
> **I raise this Creature of Wine,**
> **dedicating it as a symbol**
> **of the high intoxicating virtue of the Spirit**
> **and offering it as a vehicle**
> **for that secret and holy force**
> **which is the very power of inspiration.**

5. Place the goblet upon the Bomos, reflect for a moment on the dedication you have made. Then, with both hands extended, palms downward over the goblet, say:

I bless you, Creature of Wine,
in the name of the All-highest.
May that which you symbolize
be realized in fullness and truth
through my work this day.

6. Contemplate the wine and bring to mind all that it repre-
    sents and the spiritual virtue with which it is now endowed.
    After a few minutes of quiet reflection, raise the goblet
    toward you and say:

I receive this alchemical draft
as symbol and vehicle of the power of divine inspiration.
May I truly receive within my soul
the virtue of this elixir,
and experience divine intoxication thereby.

7. Consume the wine, then spend a few more minutes in
    contemplation.
8. Conclude the rite with the Calyx.

13

PRACTICAL MAGICK

Practical magick is, well, practical. That is to say, these are magical rites that are designed to have an effect on this plane of existence. If you perform a rite to attract money, find love, or obtain a promotion, these are examples of practical magick. Most of the spells carried down to us through the ages are in the category of practical magick.

It is common to hear or read that practical magick is somehow less spiritual than so-called high magick. Such opinions, however, only betray the magical level of the speaker. This material world is infused throughout with spirit and light. This plane of existence is necessary to the balance of all things. What is the point of a model of the four worlds of manifestation if not to manifest somewhere?

The key to these rites may be found in the Qabalistic idea of the four worlds. Practical magick works by influencing these threads of manifestation from Yetzirah to Assiah, and this is an awesome power indeed. Through visualization and other work you have already done, you have learned to create images, dreams, and emotions on the astral plane. Through the use of rites of practical magick, these astral creations are woven into the physical realities of this plane. At higher levels of magical practice and accomplishment, one may also influence the manifestation of divine archetypes into Yetzirah, and thereby to Assiah, participating actively in the moment-by-moment re-creation of the cosmos itself.

DOES PRACTICAL MAGICK WORK?

It is natural to doubt the effectiveness of practical magick. After all, we have all intently wished for something we have not obtained. We have spontaneously invented rites that should have brought the love of one we desired, or the money we needed to pay an overdue bill. Practical magick works, yet most of these attempts fail to bring the desired result. Why? More often than not, these spontaneous "rites" have suffered from one or more basic problems. Some of the more common problems follow.

The rite was not well focused: A few years ago in the United States, the Abundance Movement began to spread in New Age communities. Thousands upon thousands chanted, prayed, and visualized abundance on a daily basis. These well-meaning people may, in fact, be single-handedly responsible for the worldwide strength of the U.S. dollar and the general trend toward prosperity in America. Yet few of them seem to be deriving much, if any, individual benefit from their practices. The reason for this is that many such visualizations, prayers, meditations, and magical rites leave out an important ingredient: direction. You must be specific about who is to benefit from the work you will do and how they will benefit. If you desire a practical result that affects you personally, be certain to place yourself in the picture. Otherwise, your magical intent and work will manifest, but you may never know when or where.

The rite was too focused: A successful rite of practical magick does nothing less than change the course of the universe. Of course, a small change, a gentle manipulation of the currents of manifestation, is possible, however many magicians simply ask too much of the universe for their level of magical ability. To perform a rite to meet your favorite author is likely to be an effective use of practical magick, provided, of course, that you really do want to meet this author and that the author is not actively trying to avoid meeting you (a form of counter-rite).

On the other hand, to perform a rite to meet your favorite author at a specific coffeehouse in your neighborhood on Thursday during your lunch hour is asking a lot of the universe. Too many threads of manifestation must be influenced to bring this specific occurrence about for the average magical rite. You are asking for specific changes in the flow of manifestation for the author, yourself, the coffeehouse, the people in the coffeehouse, your entire neighborhood, the traffic situation. Indeed, it is staggering to consider how many things in the universe must happen in a particular way to bring about such a specific intent. Moreover, each of these threads has its own inertia. The magical force raised by your rite is quickly dispersed in an attempt to move so many threads.

The rite was built from the bottom up, instead of from the top down: Most wishing suffers from this problem. We wish that a certain event will occur, even wish with great intensity. Then look upward in the hope that someone or something else will grant the wish. Magical rites are based on the principle of descent through the worlds of manifestation. The rite must create the event, object, or idea on the levels above this one in the certain knowledge that what has been created *must* manifest in the worlds below.

The magician made no effort to manifest the goal: This is a common problem. Practical magick can help you obtain a promotion at work, but it cannot cause a completely unqualified person to be promoted to a position for which they are not ready. Practical magick can bring money into your life, but not if you simply sit in your house waiting for a check to arrive in the mail.

Aleister Crowley once wrote, "Every intentional act is a magical act."[1] This is an important concept. If you use practical magick to assist your case in a lawsuit, it is no less magical to hire good attorneys and to do any and all the paperwork and detective work necessary to bring about the desired result. In fact, each and every so-called mundane task, when coupled with the magical intent of your rite, is a powerful magical act.

BUILDING A RITE OF PRACTICAL MAGICK

Imagine that you work in a large professional office. Across from your desk, you have a view into the manager's office, an office you hope one day will be yours. You read on the company bulletin board that the manager is retiring, and you feel you deserve to be promoted to that office. You decide to use practical magick to tip the scales in your favor.

All practical magick (indeed all magick) begins with a clear idea of the desired goal. We then look upon the goal to determine which energies and systems of symbolism operate upon it. For example, is your goal the money (earth) a promotion will bring, the happiness (water) of having the position and title, or perhaps you need to pass a test (air) to qualify for the position? Understand your desire, your motivations, and the intended manifestation in detail. With a clear idea of the goal, and a clearly worded statement of it, you may begin to design a rite to achieve it. Remember, a rite of magick is only effective to the extent that you have clear intent.

In this case, you want the position for its interest: the work is more interesting than your current position, and calls for a better use of your abilities and training. You desire the mental challenge, and you are more than up to it. Thus, looking back to chapter 10, this rite becomes a rite of air.

The rite itself will have six basic parts. This is a general outline that is appropriate for most elemental works of practical magick.

1. Divination
2. Preparation of the chamber
3. Warding and invocation
4. Statement or visualization of the intent
5. Charging the intent
6. Closing

Before the Rite

Magicians have historically performed a divination before any rite of practical magick. A divination prior to a rite serves two purposes. First, it helps the magician make ethical decisions about a rite, as we saw in chapter 3. Second, it helps sort out the best time to perform a rite of practical magick, for, while we may make our best calculations regarding the time and place for the rite, it may be that another time or place will give an even better result. This is an important point. A negative divination regarding a planned rite does not necessarily indicate that the rite itself is wrong, but may only indicate that the time is not propitious. As you progress in your divinatory skill, you will be able to tell the difference between these answers.

While the tarot is the grand book of images for Western magick, as a divinatory tool, it often gives answers that are less than crystal clear and that require further thought and investigation. Sometimes, we just need a few simple and quick yes-or-no answers before a practical rite. An excellent tool for such acquiring answers is the pendulum.

A pendulum is any object suspended from a string, chain, or thread of sufficient length that it may swing freely. The suspended object can be anything at all: a crystal, a stone, a piece of wood, or a brass or glass pendulum specially made for the purpose. Each is equally effective, though, over time, you will find that different materials lend themselves to different questions. One artisan at Lapis Lazuli uses a tiny silver rosebud at the end of a red silk thread as her primary pendulum. Another uses a simple lead fishing weight at the end of monofilament line. Yet another uses a pearl earring that belonged to her grandmother, a witch. Personally, I often use my magical ring, suspended from about twelve inches of black sewing thread.

Select a pendulum. Between uses, keep it wrapped in black silk and store it where you keep your other magical tools. With a pendulum, many divinatory tasks are possible. In fact, the use of the pendulum forms an entire short course in advanced divination at Lapis Lazuli. The first task in that course is to use the pendulum to answer simple questions with "yes," "no," or "I don't know."

Pendulum Divination

In each and every divinatory rite involving a pendulum, it is important first to establish communication between yourself and the device. We call this "tuning the pendulum."

Begin by holding the pendulum suspended before you. Still the movements of your hand until the pendulum ceases all movement. Close your eyes, and visualize the pendulum dangling from your hand. With your eyes closed, say: **Show me "yes"** (or ask a question that has a known affirmative answer) and wait. Soon the pendulum will begin to move. When you sense this, open your eyes and note the direction of movement.

Stop the pendulum again and, with closed eyes, reestablish the visualization. Say: **Show me "no"** (or ask a question that has a known negative answer) and again wait. The pendulum will begin to move in a different manner. When you sense this, open your eyes and note again the direction of movement.

Repeat this a third time, saying: **Show me "I don't know"** (or ask an impossible question) and record the type of movement associated with this response. The energies contacted by a pendulum change depending on the place and situation, and many have limited realms of knowledge about our world. Don't be frustrated by an "I don't know" answer to a question: your pendulum is not omniscient.

In my own pendulum work, a "yes" is normally a to-and-fro movement, away and toward my body; "no" is a side-to-side swinging; "I don't know" is movement in a circle. Your own responses may differ. In fact, they may differ each time you use the pendulum. Once you have established the language through which you can communicate with it, your pendulum has been tuned.

After tuning the pendulum, frame a question or series of questions to be answered. As a very general example, your procedure might sound like this:

Should I perform this rite of practical magick now?

(Pendulum answers yes.)

Would this rite of practical magick be more effective at another time?

(Pendulum answers no.)

With this information in hand, you may confidently begin the rite.

Preparation of the Chamber

It is in the preparation of the Chamber of Art that your earlier work with correspondences and symbols comes into play. Create a Chamber of Art that reflects in every way the nature of the rite. For a rite of air, decorate the chamber in yellow and purple, choose yellow candles for light and sandalwood incense, and cover the Bomos with a yellow or purple drape. Make an airy temple of your Chamber of Art with objects, colors, and scents that connect you to the element of air. Perform your rite in the morning, the time of air. Open the windows, if possible, and let the morning breeze stir the air in your chamber.

Warding and Invocation

As for all rites of magick, begin by establishing the rhythmic breath, as you did for the earlier meditation.

For the Warding, you already have tools at hand: the Circle of Light Rite or the Setting of the Wards. All rites must begin with such a Warding to clear the air and make room for the magical act about to be performed, and to ensure that the influences upon the rite are limited to those you have invited. Execute your chosen Warding rite deliberately and carefully, and avoid undue concentration on your magical intent. You want the statement of intent to have force and emotion when stated. If you focus on the intent too early, it may dull later statements of it.

Next, having cleared your circle of all energies but that light you have drawn down, strengthen your rite by inviting powers, energies, elements, and/or deities to attend your work. These powers must be in harmony with the nature of the rite. For this rite, simple invocations of the entities and energies in question are all that are required. Incorporate magical language, borrowed from poetry or song lyrics or chants, each chosen to inspire you and turn your thoughts toward the chosen element. For this example, I have chosen a modification of a call to the elemental powers from an Aurum Solis document:

> From the East, the place of Morning Light, cometh the rushing of the wind wherein the Spirits of Air do dwell, and from which cometh the airy winds that stir to life the thoughts of all upon the earth. I call upon you, Powers of Air and Airy Sylphs, to attend to my purpose this day.

Speak this carefully and with resonance in your magical voice. Light the yellow candles and the sandalwood incense.

Statement or Visualization of Intent

While the creation of a visualization or wording of the intent should employ all of the abilities you have developed in this course of study, the rest of the rite should be done for its own sake. Once you have stated your intent, you do not need to state it again and again. The rest of the rite becomes an underscore and sealing of the intent, riding along on magical tension created by the statement or initial visualization. As Order documents explain:

> This introduces a fundamental magical principle: when once an initial declaration of Intent has been made in the opening of a rite, concentration upon that intention is to be sedulously avoided. Attention to each element of a rite, perfecting each for its own sake in its due sequence—the speeches for their splendor, the movements for their grace, the battery for its rhythm, and so on—this, carried by the initial impetus of the Declaration, is the basis of success in ceremonial working.

In this case, we choose a visualization of the intent. Visualization is far more useful than vocalization in most matters of practical magick. Visualize your goal as if seeing a photograph of the scene. Use several cycles of breath to visualize the picture fully, with sights, sounds, smells, and other sensory features of the scene. Be sure to place yourself in the picture, if appropriate to the intent. Do not visualize passing qualifying examinations, interviews, or other intermediate steps in your scene, only the finished product of your work, the accomplished goal.

Charging the Intent

Your visualiztion has created an image on the astral plane. Now charge this image to fix it and create the energy necessary to bring forth its manifestation. On a deep inbreath, draw down light from above, as you did in the Circle of Light rite. On the outbreath, visualize this light flowing from within you to surround the image, until the scene is circled and brightly lit by the light. Repeat this technique three times, strengthening the light and the visualization with each repetition.

Closing

Let this visualization fade from your consciousness and release the powers invoked, thanking them for their participation. Again, simple language is suitable:

> Spirits and Powers of Air, be there peace between us. With the blessing of the All-Highest return to your abodes and with gladness come again when you are called.

Let your visualization of the Wards fade from your consciousness, dissolving your circle and stepping into the world, confident that, even now, you and your goal are rushing toward one another in space and time.

Note this rite in your notebook with the date, time, and other particulars. When you achieve your goal, note this as well. Later, such information may be used to formulate your own book of magical principles, the methods and language and gestures that work best for you and have proven effective. The great magical texts of the past, guarded so carefully by each magician, were little more than this. For the artisan of Magick, to know oneself through experiment and analysis is to gain great power.

After the Rite

After finishing your rite, it is common to worry about your goal, to have doubts that you will achieve it, plan other rites to make up for what you believe this one may have lacked, or endlessly draw tarot cards to gain a glimpse into how things are progressing. Each of these actions is a magical act that works in direct opposition to your rite, weakening it. Hidden in each of these actions is the seed of doubt. With your frequent attention, these actions will grow into a mighty force against your intent.

Likewise, to brag about your rite or tell others of what you have done difuses the magical energy of your work. Moreover, talking with others about a rite may also weaken it, as those listening add their own emotional, intellectual, and magical energy to the pure energy you labored to achieve. Have faith in the power of your higher self, and in the power of your rite. The very laws of the cosmos, the physics of manifestation, will bring about your result if only you will work with them. As the Taoists say, the person who lives in harmony with the Tao may, through not doing, accomplish all things.

MORE PRACTICAL MAGICK: FINDING LOST OBJECTS

One statistic often quoted is that we spend, on average, approximately two years of our lives searching for lost objects. This rite of practical magick may not shorten the time you spend conducting such searches, but it's certainly a more enjoyable way to spend that time, and may perhaps have a greater value than simply finding the lost objects themselves.

The principles of this rite are similar to those of the preceding rite. This rite, however, requires an exploration of another magical concept: the holographic nature of the four worlds.

A holograph is a picture that captures, in two dimensions, a three-dimensional image. These lifelike images are made with the aid of a laser. If you hold a holograph at the proper angle, you will see the three-dimensional image. Holographs portray the object so realistically that you may walk completely around the image, viewing it from all sides. More remarkable still, even very small pieces of certain types of holographic film carry all the information recorded by the whole film. Thus, if you break one of these holographic plates in half, you get two complete three-dimensional images.

The magical universe is much the same. Assiah, the world of manifestation, is a projected image from the worlds above. It is infused with the light that connects all things. Every infinitely small piece of the manifest cosmos contains an image of, and map to, the entire cosmos. This is an important concept in magick, one often cloaked in mystery and symbolic language. It is the point at which some aspects of science and magick come close to one another, the first more interested in theory and understanding, the latter more interested in use and application.[2]

Knowing that every part of our universe contains a map of and connection to the rest of the universe, in magical terms, our question becomes: How do we access this map? We have already developed the tools needed to do this: visualization and focus. We need only apply them in a structured manner. In this case, the structure is a physical map.

Every good legend has a map somewhere in the story. From the first human attempts to record journeys in a way that others could follow, such as early cave paintings, maps have contained not only directional information, but also representations of impressions that the mapmaker hopes to relate. "Beyond here be dragons," an old map reads, communicating a natural fear of the unknown. "X marks the treasure," another tells us, charting a path into an adventure story.

While maps have progressed from storytelling devices to tools of navigation and science, they continue to have some rather curious features. I recently used a map of New York to discover the best route from my apartment to my workplace in the hope of finding a faster, more direct route. As I pored over the map and familiar street names passed beneath my fingers, another part of my mind visualized the journey in some considerable detail. My mind used these images to organize various streets, street corners, and subway stops into a memory of a trip that I had never actually taken. Actually walking the route had an odd sense of familiarity, though I had never walked that particular route before. This may seem obvious and we may take this feature of maps for granted, yet it is rather remarkable that a simple, two-dimensional representation of a place, showing but a few sketchy details, can serve as a guide to the actual place. It is by this same faculty of mind that other representational systems, such as Qabalistic correspondences, may be mastered and used.

To use a map in a divination, it is important to realize that every map is accurate. The map either shows an accurate representation of a consensus reality, such as the location of a subway stop, or it shows an accurate representation of the mapmaker's impression of the place, and perhaps even his or her state of mind. There is considerable power in the comprehension of this concept, for it is a tool that may be applied to great advantage. Art, for example, becomes not only a representation of a thought, emotion, person, or place, but also a map showing paths that may be followed into realms unknown.

As a simple exploration of this concept, we will use a map as a divinatory tool to find a lost object. For the rite below, obtain or draw a map of the area in which you believe the object may be found. This may be a drawing of the rooms in your house, or a map of your neighborhood. Later in your magical development, other types of maps may be used, such as tarot cards, sigils, or works of art. It is best to begin simply, however, with a physical map of a physical place. You will also need a felt-tip pen or other marker.

A Rite of Divination for Finding Lost Objects

This rite employs several of the principles discussed so far, and follows the basic structure for a rite given in chapter 9.

Preparation of the Chamber: Divination is more easily accomplished if distractions are kept to a minimum. Darken your Chamber of Art and light several candles, enough to allow you to read the map. Light jasmine incense, or another incense associated with the Moon or divination. Put on your robe and ring, and light the lamp. Place the map upon the Bomos.

Warding and Invocation: Perform either the Circle of Light rite or the Setting of the Wards.

Statement or Visualization of the Intent: Facing east, assume a Wand stance, then raise your arms in a Tau, palms down. Slowly turning your palms upward, quiet your thoughts, and focus on a visualization of the lost object. Assume a mental attitude of open receptivity. Your visualization forms a connection between the lost object and your rite, bringing to life the map on your Bomos.

The Divination: Stand or sit with the Bomos before you, facing east. While holding the image of the lost object firmly in mind, pass your hand slowly over the map. Use slow, methodical side-to-side motions, with your hand one or two inches above the map surface. Open yourself to a sense of the currents that flow beneath your hand: currents of light, currents of warmth and coolness. When you feel this, maintain a visualization of the lost object and locate the warmest place or places on the map. Using the marker, mark the the map to indicate these locations.

Turn the map 90 degrees. With your eyes closed, repeat the divination. If you find the same places this time as before, your divination is complete. If not, turn the map again and strengthen your visualization of the lost object. Then proceed as above until you can consistently find the same one or two places.

Closing: Return to a Wand posture, facing east. Allow the visualization of your Wards to fade, and spend a few moments meditating upon the answers revealed by your divination. Extinguish the lamp.

After the Rite: Seek the lost object in the place or places indicated on your map. There you will find them, or find something or someone associated with the lost object that helps you locate it.

14

TIMES AND TIDES

Part of magical study that goes far beyond the intellectual is the growing understanding of the tides and rhythms of our Earth and the energies around us. All of creation turns in patterns, rhythms, and tides, from galaxies that spin in circular patterns together in the blackness of space, to the ebb and flow of the lunar tides each month; from the dance of the planets through the stars and our psyches, to the squirrel who knows instinctively when to begin the storage of food for the oncoming winter. As modern humans, we have distanced ourselves from the rhythm of nature. Winter seems to come as a surprise to those who live in northern climates, though it comes each and every year. We are moody during the New Moon, without ever considering that this happens to us each month.

In fact, the subtle influences of the cosmos are around us and within us during every moment of our existence. We grow in both wisdom and power as we come to understand these flows and cycles of energy and influence. To understand them intellectually is not sufficient; we must begin to feel these powers instinctively and plumb them for the myriad associations and correspondences they bring.

To tailor our magical practice, for example, to avoid works of practical magick during the winter is not a weakness on the part of the magician during these months, but a great statement of strength that we have taken these tides within us and drawn them into our magick, along with all the power they bring.

THE SEASONAL TIDES: FIRE FESTIVALS AND SUN FESTIVALS

Fire festivals are celebrations drawn from old Celtic thought. The Celts actually recognized just three seasons each year, but there were four annual festivals that involved the lighting of fires to mark the division of seasons. Eventually, these were adapted to the Roman calendar of four seasons and are celebrated to this day. Among many pagans and Wiccans, these days are the high feast days of the year, also called "greater sabbats."

While the fire festivals were and are today magical observances of considerable power, they lack the power inherent in the Sun festivals. These are the days marking the actual transitions of balance as the Sun moves through the seasons. The Sun festivals have an abundance of magical correspondences and symbolism.

The fire festivals are undoubtedly colorful and more suited to festive gatherings, while the Sun festivals are better suited to magical work and can have an impact on your magical activities. At Lapis Lazuli, we celebrate the entire eight-spoked Wheel of the Year.

Winter Solstice: Tempus Eversionis

In the Aurum Solis tradition, the year is magically divided into four quarters, each corresponding to a season and each with a purpose and character of its own. With Winter Solstice, on December 21st, comes the quarter *Tempus Eversionis,* the Tide of Conflict, also referred to as the Tide of Overturning. This is a time when no works of practical magick are attempted, yet during which personal spiritual development continues.

Tempus Eversionis is a time when we draw within, as the Sun has withdrawn from the world, and give way to the nature of the Earth in winter. While some animals hibernate and others snuggle themselves into cozy homes with gathered winter food supplies, we also turn away from much of our magical activity, beginning activities that strengthen us and increase our devotion to the light. It is a time to focus on meditations and any religious activities in which you may engage. Study more, read more, and strengthen ties with friends and family.

The day of the Solstice is a time to recognize the transition from one set of activities and one outlook on life to another. It is also the darkest and shortest day of the year. Yet, in the midst of this darkness is always the promise of spring, the knowledge that the Sun will return in time. The best celebrations of this holiday are those revolving around candles, symbolizing the theme of light within darkness.

Imbolc

Also called Oimelc or Candlemas, this holiday is usually celebrated beginning at sundown on February 1st and lasting until sundown on February 2nd. Literally, *Imbolc* means "in the belly of the Mother," referring to the seeds of potential growth lying dormant under frozen winter ground, in "Mother" Earth. *Oimelc*, means "milk of ewes." It is the beginning of the old traditional lambing season. This holiday is said to be sacred to the old Celtic fire goddess, Brigit, patron of smithcraft, healing, midwifery, and poetry.

The celebration of Imbloc is similar to that of the Winter Solstice. Light candles or lamps in each room of your house right after sunset to honor the rebirth of the Sun, which at this time of the year, is just noticeable during our Solar Adordations.

Spring Equinox: **Tempus Sementis**

At the Spring Equinox, we will enter the quarter *Tempus Sementis*, the Tide of Stimulation and the Tide of Planting or Sowing. This is a time for beginning new things, a time to do new works, a time to plant new seeds that will be appreciated fully at a later harvest. This tide reaches its fullness at Beltaine (on or near May 1st), the great celebration of fertility, growth, and love.

Beltaine

Beltaine is one of the oldest festivals celebrated with feasts and magical rites, usually on May 1st. The word *Beltaine* means "fire of Bel," Belinos being one name for the Sun god who is coronated on this day. With the onset of summer, weather becomes warmer and the world blossoms with growth. In Celtic traditions, this was a time of unabashed sexuality and promiscuity during which marriages of a year and a day could be undertaken, though these observations are less common today. Historically, young people spent an entire night in the woods and fields a-maying, their sexual energies directed toward fertilization of the fields for the growth of crops and other plants. In Germany, the day was known as the feast of Saint Walpurga, or Walpurgisnacht.

Traditionally, people rose at the first light of dawn to go outdoors and gather flowers and branches to decorate their homes on this day. Women braided flowers into their hair. Men and women alike decorated their bodies.

Summer Solstice: **Tempus Messis**

On or near June 21st, the Summer Solstice begins the quarter *Tempus Messis*, the Tide of Completion, or, as it is also known, the Tide of Harvest. This is the quarter of the year given to works of practical magick, including such activities as sphereworking, evocations, consecrations, astral travel, and scrying. The seed that was planted in the Tempus Sementis has now thrust itself above ground, growing quickly toward harvest. There is much to learn in the course of this tide to prepare for the harvest of the work. Learn well the beginnings of Tempus Sementis and the workings of Tempus Messis, until they are part of your very self. For seeds shallowly planted or scattered on a rocky surface will not flourish.

Lughnasadh/Lammas
July 31st–August 1st

Lughnasadh means "the funeral games of Lugh," the Celtic Sun god. Traditionally, it was celebrated on either July 31st or August 1st. The god hosted these funeral games in honor of his foster mother, *Tailte*. In some Celtic, traditions Tailtean craft fairs and Tailtean year-and-a-day marriages are celebrated on this day. In nature, this is the time when the plants of spring wither and drop their fruits or seeds in preparation for the coming winter and to ensure growth in the spring. Christianity expressed this harvest theme with Lammas, meaning "loaf-mass," a day during which newly baked loaves of bread are placed on the altar.

Fall Equinox: Tempus Consilii

On or near September 21st, the Fall Equinox ushers in the quarter *Tempus Consilii*, the Tide of Quiessence, also called the Tide of Reflection. This is the time of the gathering, the harvest of the spiritual activities seeded in Tempus Sementis and brought to fruition during Tempus Messis. While bringing life to new works and great workings of practical magick are characteristic of the previous two tides, this tide is a time to begin the reaping and evaluation of that work. This is also the tide in which works of trimming or reduction are most appropriate, a time to let go of that which has served its purpose in our lives. As the tide turns past Samhain, the magical curriculum should increasingly turn to the finishing up of magical works started earlier in the year, in preparation for the restful, regenerative Tempus Eversionis.

Samhain

Samhain is a word meaning "end of summer." Traditionally, Samhain represented the third and final harvest of the year and was celebrated on October 31st, although November 1st was also used. This and Beltaine are spirit nights, a time when the veil between the worlds is at its very thinnest, and spiritualist communications with ancestors and departed loved ones is easiest.

In ancient times, this feast of the dead was celebrated by placing food offerings on altars and doorsteps for the wandering dead and spirits. Single candles were lit and left in windows to help guide the spirits of ancestors and loved ones. Extra chairs were placed at dinner tables for unseen guests. Traveling after dark was not advised, as spirits and wee folk were about and likely to be most playful and troublesome.

LUNAR TIDES

The lunar tides correspond to the phases of the Moon, changing four times each month. These tides have a powerful impact on our emotional world and upon the tides of both the seas on Earth and the fluids within us. Women, in particular, are especially sensitive to these tidal changes each month, which is not to say that the lunar tides are more important to women than to men. It is rather a statement that men, who often ignore or even deny the flow of lunar tides, have much more work to do in this aspect of Sophia Terrae.

With regard to the timing and performance of magical rites, the Full Moon is the time of greatest magical power.

The first-quarter Moon is given best to works of beginnings and growth. During the waning Moon of the third quarter, planners of magical operations in the first week need only keep in mind that the influence of the Moon on their work is less than full. Also, this is a time to consider works of reduction and release of something in your life, as your rite may "ride the wave" of the waning Moon.

The last few days of the crescent Moon, however, are a time to take care in your operations. As an Order document states:

the last visible stages of the wane ... tend to be malefic and are under the power of Hecate.

Practical magick should be suspended during the New Moon, as the power of the Moon is not merely dark during this time, but highly unstable. The balancing of the forces necessary to bring a rite to magical fruition is far more difficult and dangerous during the New Moon. Yet the New Moon has a great and dark power of her own that is profoundly magical, and is worthy of exploration for students well-grounded in the Earth.

The strength of the lunar tides also fluctuates from one season to another. The New Moon is at its most magical in the spring, while the Full Moon is at the height of her power in fall.[1]

THE VELOCIA

Tides of great importance to Aurum Solis are the *Velocia*, taken from the great Sanskrit traditions of the East. These are fluctuations in the Earth's odic mantle. This mantle is made up of two essences: the collection of life-forces from all living things on Earth, and the vast inorganic mantle of the Earth's geomagnetic fields. These tides flow from east to west, and are five in number (see Table 12, page 217). They are calculated quite simply: the flow begins from sunrise and the cycle of all five is completed in two hours, beginning with the Tattva of Akasha and progressing as shown in Table 12. Each tide lasts for twenty-four minutes.

A rite begun in one Tattva will remain in the energy of this tide once the circle is sealed, as is accomplished with the Circle of Light rite or the Setting of the Wards. This is another reason that warding rites are important to magical ceremonies. Without them, a rite

Table 12. The Velocia.

TATTVIC SYMBOL	TATTVA	ELEMENT
Indigo Ovoid	Akasha	Spirit
Blue Disk	Vayu	Air
Red Triangle	Agni	Fire
White Crescent	Apas	Water
Yellow Square	Prithivi	Earth

of fire, for example, would have to be started and finished within twenty-four minutes! The mechanics of this is that, once the circle is sealed with a warding rite and appropriate invocations of spiritual force have been made, the working develops its own magical current in harmony with the external currents during which it was begun. Thus, a rite involving fire energies, once begun, picks up an internal magical current of fire and the external world may proceed as it will while we complete our magical work.

PLANETARY HOURS

In more advanced Aurum Solis workings, planetary hours are of great importance, but for general workings, the Velocia have a much greater and more immediate influence on the subtle aspects of a magical rite.

Still, the planetary hours can be important to a rite, or at least contributory to its success in some cases. The character of the planets is deeply buried in the consciousness of us all, and the planetary hours have influence to coax responses from our psyches in accordance with planetary archetypes in our shared unconscious. We know without any magical training, for instance, that Venus is the planet of love and amorous activities, that Mars is a planet of war and aggression. From our Solar Adorations, we have a closer understanding of how each planet factors into our magical work, while an appreciation of the tides of the Moon will gives us considerable insight into the character of this threefold goddess.

The calculation of planetary hours must begin with an understanding of the magical hour. Planetary hours are calculated from sunrise to sunset, and again from sunset to sunrise, with twelve even divisions made between each of these events. Thus, a magical hour is not sixty minutes in length at all times, nor is the magical night equal in length to the magical day, except twice each year during the Equinoxes. To calculate the magical hour for the day requires only a knowledge of the times of sunrise and sunset and a little bit of arithmetic. As the length of the magical hour will not vary widely over the course of a few days, the calculation of the magical hour may generally be done just once a week.

For example, if, on a particular day, the Sun rises at 4:58 A.M. and sets at 7:02 P.M., local time, clearly this day is at some time after the Spring Equinox, when the days are longer than the nights, but before Fall Equinox. The period of daylight is fourteen hours and four minutes, or 844 minutes (14 hours times 60 minutes each, plus 4). Divide this number by 12 and you arrive at a magical hour of 70 minutes.[2] Without recalculating, it may easily be seen that the magical hour during the following night will be 50 minutes (the two taken together: daytime magical hour + nighttime magical hour will always equal 120 minutes. In this case, if the daytime hour is 70 minutes, then the nighttime hour is 120 minutes minus 70 minutes, or 50 minutes).

Once you know this, you must also know the planetary attribution for the day: Sun for Sunday, Moon for Monday, Mars for Tuesday, Mercury for Wednesday, Jupiter for Thursday, Venus for Friday, and Saturn for Saturday. In our example, we will assume that this calculation is for a Monday, and the planetary association is with the Moon.

To calculate the planetary hours for this day, generate a chart showing each planet's influence lasting 67 minutes from sunrise, beginning with the planetary association for the day. Table 13 shows the progressions.

The creation of such a table is actually quite easy using a reference chart similar to that shown in Table 14 (page 220), which indicates, for any given day of the week, the attribution of planetary hours for that day. All that is left is for you to calculate the

Table 13. Example Progression of Planetary Hours.

MAGICAL HOUR	BEGINS AT CLOCK TIME	PLANETARY ATRTRIBUTION
1	4: 58 A.M.	Moon
2	6:08 A.M.	Saturn
3	7:18 A.M.	Jupiter
4	8:28 A.M.	Mars
5	9:38 A.M.	Sun
6	10:48 A.M.	Venus
7	11:58 A.M.	Mercury
8	1:08 P.M.	Moon
9	2:18 P.M.	Saturn
10	3:28 P.M.	Jupiter
11	4:38 P.M.	Mars
12	5:48 P.M.	Sun

length of a magical hour and construct a table similar to Table 13 to determine the hour corresponding to your intended magical rite.

Though this process may look complicated, the calculation and creation of charts for planetary hours is actually quite simple once you get the hang of it. Practice and familiarity are the keys to success, as in all things magical.

Table 14. Reference Chart for the Planetary Hours.

MON	TUE	WED	THU	FRI	SAT	SUN	HOURS
Moon	Mars	Mercury	Jupiter	Venus	Saturn	Sun	1,8,15,22
Saturn	Sun	Moon	Mars	Mercury	Jupiter	Venus	2,9,16,23
Jupiter	Venus	Saturn	Sun	Moon	Mars	Mercury	3,10,17,24
Mars	Mercury	Jupiter	Mars	Saturn	Sun	Moon	4,11,18
Sun	Moon	Mars	Mercury	Jupiter	Venus	Saturn	5,12,19
Venus	Saturn	Sun	Moon	Mars	Mercury	Jupiter	6,13,20
Mercury	Jupiter	Venus	Saturn	Sun	Moon	Mars	7,14,21

Ritual Planning

Though we have discussed several influential tides for a working, most rites use just three: the solar tide, the lunar tide, and the Velocia. The planetary hours have influence primarily in rites devoted to a planetary archetype and in some Qabalistic rites. For general workings, however, the planetary hour is a dimly sensed influence, having little real impact on the effectiveness of the rite.

The timing of rites to coincide with appropriate tides is, however, crucial to magical practice and study. In your magical work from this point on, you should make a habit of knowing the tides for the work, especially for works of practical magick, and become accustomed to the subtle influences these lend to your efforts.

While it is true that any magical rite may be performed at any time by a sufficiently practiced and confident magician, to do so is much like running up the down escalator. It can be done, but the work is that much more difficult as you draw from other sources the power that would have been available with the tide. A rite of magical growth and inception may be successfully done during a New Moon of the Tempus Eversionis, but, were the same rite done with the same degree of effort at the proper time, the results would be dramatic in scope.

15

A FEW LAST THOUGHTS

As I write this final chapter, it is September and the first signs of fall are upon the winds. Trees have not yet changed color, but the Sun moves inexorably on and the energies are shifting even now, especially in the morning light and at twilight. The breeze stirs leaves outside my window to life and sets them dancing on the autumn air in the last joyful dances of summer.

In these pages, we have touched on many ideas and learned new ways to view the world around us. You have stretched your thoughts to encompass the mysteries of the Qabalah, and turned your eyes to the inner workings of nature. Most important, you have learned that you cannot step away from a study of magick without the certain knowledge that there is very much more to your idea of who you are than perhaps you once thought. In fact, you cannot step away from a study of magick at all, for the very experience of these ideas and symbols has changed you forever.

Yet all of this is for naught if this learning remains a matter of tables built, pages read and paragraphs quoted. My entire study of magick and mystery, of art and life, of elements and stars, is at its finest in the happy melange of symbols, thoughts, and emotions that accompanies those leaves that dance outside my window.

For magick, as a study and as a way of life, lends a certain subtle coloring to the simplest of nature's displays, bringing to life this September day. It brings a joyful wonder at each moment of time, and a peaceful strength that comes of unity with the realms both above and within, both out there and right here.

Magick as a way of life brings the playful hint that these leaves stirring in this wind, in the shifting energies of Earth and Sun, have something yet to teach me that I will find in no book. I leave you now to follow them and bid you do the same, for, as we part after this journey together, I give you one last secret of magick, the elixir of the Hero: Everything Is Magick.

> O my friends, live your lives happily, far from narrowness. Live happy. It was the happiness of heaven that created you; and with a kind of laughter, that is, with a dilating, a movement, a splendor, it declared you, as if it were rollicking.[1]

APPENDIX A: AURUM SOLIS AND THE OGDOADIC TRADITION

The word *Ogdoadic* means "pertaining to the number eight." It is a rather new word, coined to group-related Western mystery traditions. While almost every single-digit number, and quite a few other numbers, have a long association with particular philosophies and religions, eight is a fascinating number that ties together several philosophical threads. The task, when looking historically at such numbers, is not merely occurrence ("Oh my gosh, stop signs have eight sides!"). Instead, we must examine cultural threads for prominence of the number and the context in which it appears.

THE OGDOADIC TRADITION: THREADS FROM A GRAND TAPESTRY

While the number eight may appear throughout art, writing, history, and across cultures, the task of examining each appearance is a tedious one. Still, we have uncovered several important historical associations. Perhaps here we can pull together a few of the threads from one corner of the Ogdoadic tapestry.

- In Mesopotamia, the number eight, sometimes represented in cuniform script, is used in the place of a deity's name, denoting divinity. It was used in art and religious practice in much the same symbolic way that the number three appeals to trinitarian Christians.

- Later, in Pythagorean philosophical thought, the number eight represented completed mathematical perfection. This was adopted by later Christians to indicate regeneration, theosis, and palingenesis.

- Valentinus, a 2nd-century Christian bishop who almost became Pope, borrowed from Gnostic ideas to postulate thirty aeons, spiritual principles separating humanity from God. The total of thirty was made up of an ogdoad (8), a decad (10), and a dodecad (12). The ogdoad is the most immediate to human existence and the most explored of these aeons, continuing to influence Gnosticism to this day. The ogdoad was made up of: depth (bythos), silence (sige), mind (nous), truth (aletheia), reason (logos), life (zoe), man (anthropos), and church (ecclesia).

- An eight-pointed star (see figure 10, page 229) or eight-petaled flower often adorns the veil of the Virgin Mary in Orthodox Christian icons. Even now, the eight-pointed star is often used as a symbol of resurrection on Greek and Syrian Orthodox Easter cards and artwork. It is the basis for several spiritual exercises used by Orthodox seminarians to explore the resurrection of Christ.

- The Western musical scale consists of seven notes, with the eighth having the same tone, though different pitch, as the first. A regeneration and rebirth of sorts takes place, and another cycle is begun. In Cicero's *The Dream of Scipio*, he links the notes of the scale to the fixed planets of ancient astronomy; As Scipio tells his grandson, '"Skilled men have imitated this harmony with string and with voices, so as to open for themselves a way of return to that region."

And to borrow inspiration from a few of the great and honored systems of the East:

- In Chinese thought, the eight trigrams of the *I Ching* make up the 64 hexagrams used for divination and as keys to wisdom. Throughout Chinese philosophy, great wisdom is thought to be associated with the number eight, or sequences and multiples of eight.
- In classical Chinese medicine, the number eight corresponds to the eight winds (these are both physical and energetic ideas), and the breath (one common translation of the word *Qi*). It is written in the *Nei Jing* and commentaries that the breath of man responds to the wind, creating the principle of inspiration in its original meaning. Life begins and ends with the breath in this system of thought and practice. As goes the body, in Chinese medical thought, so goes the mind; as goes the mind, so go the spirits, finding inspiration and aspiration in the winds.
- In many of the programmed sequences of movements in Chinese martial arts and *Qi Gong* (called forms), the total movements add up to multiples of eight. This number represents the fullness of humankind on Earth, and is one number shy of nine, the fullness of heaven.

In his book, *The Tarot*, Paul Foster Case devotes a chapter to the "Occult Meaning of Numbers." About the number eight, he wrote:

It is the only figure except 0 which may be written over and over again without lifting pen from paper. Thus, in mathematics the figure 8, written horizontally, is the sign of infinity. Among its occult meanings are:

Rhythm, alternate cycles of involution and evolution, vibration, flux and reflux and the like. It represents also the fact that opposite forms of expression (that is, all pairs of opposites) are effects of a single Cause. (See, on this point, Isaiah 45, verses 5 to 7.)

This number 8 is the digit value of the name IHVH (Jehovah), 888 is the numeration of the name Jesus in Greek, and 8 is not only the "Dominical Number," or "Number of the Lord," in Christian numeral symbolism, but is also the particular number of the god called Thoth by Egyptians, Nebo by Assyrians, Hermes by Greeks, and Mercury by Romans. Thus 8 is pre-eminently the number of magick and of Hermetic science.[1]

There are many more such occurrences of things Ogdoadic, always with the digit eight positioned as a primary number of wisdom, regeneration, or both. In the Aurum Solis tradition, the number eight, in the form of the eight-pointed star, is our great symbol of regeneration, magical attainment, and new life, pulling together these threads in one powerful and great symbol (see figure 10, page 229). The eight-pointed star is of paramount importance to the Order.

Figure 10. The eight-pointed star.

Initiates of Aurum Solis, who stand as heirs to these diverse traditions, place an interpretation upon the Glorious Star of Regeneration which reconciles both spiritual and earthly goals. To live effectively, whether for the sake of this world or to speed us upon our inward Way of Return, is alike dependent upon our effort, day by day, to realize our potential. "To find our True Will and do it" is the sum of every aspiration: but both the finding and the performance need trained and ready faculties. The path of high magick fulfills these needs. No effort is in vain, no experience fruitless: everything helps us towards our goal.[2]

You will understand and appreciate the placement of this symbol in Order practice as you progress.

One version of the Aurum Solis Rite of Integration, the second initiatory rite of the Order, explains the Ogdoadic Tradition as follows:

> Hear now, O Theourgos, concerning the works and the life of the Glorious Star.
>
> The primary symbols of the Ogdoadic Tradition are the Fivefold Pattern of the House of Sacrifice and the Eightfold Star of Regeneration. The arcana of the House of Sacrifice are a key at once to the dynamism of the universe, and to that patter in the Divine Mind in accord with which human nature has come into being. This same key is also, therefore, that by which the faculties of the psyche are evoked in their true and potent order, and likewise it is that key by which the hidden powers of the universe can be understood, realized and attained. Above the image of the House of Sacrifice shines forth the glorious symbol which both fulfills and transcends it: the Eightfold Star of Regeneration. The Eightfold Star, which has been employed from ancient times to represent Life Divine, is the ensign of attainment and the emblem of an undying aspiration; and, supremely, it betokens that ultimate act of Regeneration whereby the Divine Mind calls back to its eternal selfhood, into the eternal Becoming which is both the essence and the act of the divine nature, everything which it has sent forth into space and time.
>
> These great emblems and the ancillary tokens of the Ogdoadic Tradition are to be found, widespread, at significant points in the art and architecture, and even in

the literature, of Europe. They are the visible signature of a living Hermetic Gnosis, of a dynamic esoteric ferment, among whose initiates have been numbered some of the most profound luminaries in the shaping of Western aspiration. For one thousand years our brethren of the Glorious Star have proclaimed the Ogdoadic mysteries in symbol and in word; yet the uninitiate, lacking the keys, have perceived therein only a canon of design or literary form. The tradition has in the wise repeatedly been revealed, even displayed to the public gaze, yet it has not been seen; our Mysteries have been proclaimed, yet remain inviolate.

If we look beyond the cultures of the West, beyond the closely interwoven fabric of European thought and history, we find, widespread through other cultures too, symbols which relate to the Ogdoadic Tradition and which, by their appropriate use, declare the knowledge and understanding of the initiate. We acknowledge and respect the schools of wisdom with which these symbols are associated, and we respect their special use and interpretation of these symbols. But, while we say assuredly that the teachings of Aurum Solis would not exclude those interpretations, we respect also their customary secrecy and we do not seek to know or elucidate further.

Know, however, O Theourgos, that in European lands the territory in which the Western Mysteries properly so called have been developed and have flourished—there are certain places in divers regions where the mighty symbols of the Ogdoadic Tradition have been emplaced in centuries past, and even now remain established: and these places are held by us to be most sacred sites of our tradition, where the power of a revered antiquity is added to the unchanging and deeply magical potency established there by means of the signs and by the will of those who wrought them.

The mysteries of the Ogdoadic Tradition were early transmitted to a number of the medieval Guilds, profoundly influencing their initiatory rites and disciplines. Thus ensued a high flowering of true Ogdoadic symbolism in art and architecture: enduring and sure tokens which bear witness to the mystical insight and elevated calling of the Guildsmen. Initiates of the Glorious Star in these latter times may look upon these Ogdoadic works, upon paintings and frescoes, upon delicate gems and great buildings, and say, "Here were my brethren."

Nobly, and with most mystical significance, was the Fivefold Pattern of the House of Sacrifice employed in the initiatory workings of our medieval brethren the Knights Templar. Therein did they most skillfully evoke and co-ordinate the functions and faculties of the psyche. Nobly too did they bear, in scarlet upon their white mantles, the Eightfold Star of Regeneration.

With arcane intent, for the creation of a sanctuary of power wherein Supernal Light might focus upon earth, did Benedetto Gaetano, high initiate of the Glorious Star, ordain the emplacement of our symbol upon the surrounding pillars of strength in Rome. For some six hundred years that mystic citadel has stood; set apart from its environs, seen but not perceived save by the initiate and the visionary, traversed but not entered save by those who hold the key of the Mysteries.

Mighty was the mystical and secret Ismaili Order of the Faithful Ones of Love which, in Asia Minor, comparably with the Sufis and Dervishes, followed within the Islamic world the path of inner illumination and of devotion to the spiritual elevation of humanity. Mighty was its Ogdoadic power; mighty were its planetary workings.

Mighty indeed was the Ogdoadic society of the Fideli d'Amore which, established in Italy at the end of the 12th century, was a Western formulation of the symbolism, mystique and practice of the Faithful Ones of Love, added to and enriched by the Order of the Temple. Notable in the development of the Fideli d'Amore through many generations was the Florentine family of Cavalcanti, in which philosophy and independence of mind formed a proud heritage. Beyond their own lives and works, the Cavalcanti have added an undying luster to the whole Western Mystery Tradition by the great minds which they have apprised of the Fideli d'Amore and brought to initiation therein. Of these initiates, two especially are outstanding: Dante Alighieri, whom the poet Guido Cavalcanti introduced to the Fideli d'Amore in the 13th century, and Marsilio Ficino, the great Renaissance philosopher and mystic, who was brought to initiation in the 15th century by Giovanni Cavalcanti as Ficino's own words attest.

In the city of Florence, in the 15th century, the Ogdoadic society called the Careggi Circle was formed from the membership of the Platonist Academy, under the inspiring genius of Marsilio Ficino, Neoplatonist scholar as well as initiate of Fideli d'Amore. Brief in earthly reckoning was its splendor but deathless its glory: none can recount the history of the making of Europe without telling of the awakening which was here wrought in the minds of men and women. The work of the Careggi Circle, in the very beginnings of the Renaissance, had effects which even yet reverberate throughout the Western world. Scholars, poets and philosophers traveled thither from afar, seeking initiation or at least the inspiration of converse with the group. Reuchlin, the pioneer German Qabalist, and Erasmus, the humanist who carried the spirit of Renaissance learning to his native Holland, were among those profoundly influenced by the initiates of Careggi. Founded initially through the philosophic and occult interests of Cosimo de Medici, Ficino's patron, it was developed brilliantly by Cosimo's grandson, Lorenzo the Magnificent, who inherited from Cosimo the initiatory name of Pan. Ficino himself, as supreme adept of the Careggi Circle, took the name of Saturnus. Guiliano de Medici, Lorenzo's brother, was Hippolytus. Pico della Mirandola, the brilliant young Qabalist, was Apollo. Angelo Poliziano, poet in three languages, was Hercules. Michelangelo Buonarotti, painter, sculptor and poet of heroic imagination, was also an initiate of this high gathering, the last before the death of Lorenzo, and the murder of several initiates of the inner ring, marked the onset of savage persecution by religious fanatics and the dispersal of the society.

High and most noble were the Ogdoadic works of the 16th-century Order of the Helmet, whose emblem betokened silence and invisibility. Its initiates wrought in glorious words a world of wonder and of awe in which the mysteries would find an honored place. Through the centuries following, and even now, the writings of these initiates give wings of fire to the aspirations of those who hear or read them, and win their hearts to the Mysteries, to seek them out and find them in truth.

These Orders and their initiates do we salute in the splendor of the Glorious Star. And so likewise do we honor their successors, the brethren of the 18th-century society of the blazing Wheel, Societas Rotae Fulgentis, who guarded the tradition for future generations, laying the foundations and preserving the sphere of amity upon which, and within which, Aurum Solis came to be established.

This, O Theourgos, is but a brief recounting of thy lineage; and herein thou mayest behold somewhat of the earthly manifestation of the High Company of the Glorious Star. Yet even were it possible to name all Orders and initiates of the Ogdoadic Tradition, even thus would the Glorious Star not appear in its fullness.

For each member on earth of this High Company strives for the Light at every level of being: physical, astral, mental and spiritual; and thus it is that through these incarnate brethren the powers of the Mystical Light are ever and continually evoked down from World to World, from level to level, to find their manifestation and realization in the world of physical being.

Yet it is not their own powers solely that these brethren channel down from those radiant Worlds wherein their inner faculties subsist. Nor in their deeds of power do they strive unaided. For the high Company of the Glorious Star is a coruscating interplay of forces which, pulsing and flashing with life, with love and with power, unceasingly—while aeons shall endure—descends through the Worlds to ascend again to imageless heights. And in its entire spiritual reality and activity this same fellowship numbers also among its participants a great and shining hierarchy in the Worlds invisible. Initiates who have passed beyond physical life, but who continue to work intimately with, to watch over, to guide and to empower the brethren on earth, their beloved children and co-workers. Some, higher still, luminous and potent discarnate ones, high Guardians of the Glorious Star, who transmit the thrilling radiance of unseen and unseeable ideas. Some, most exalted, scarcely to be distinguished from the divine effulgence which encompasses them: they whose vital impulse and essence is the very life-current and foundation of the work of the Glorious Star. And, at every level of the invisible hierarchy, beings too of an entirely spiritual quality, who have never known incarnation, and who participate in the greater Fraternity according as its modalities and purposes correspond to their nature.

Into all this luminous texture of being and action, the brethren on earth of the Glorious Star are initiated;

and thou, O Theourgos, art one of this high Company. Thine be the Power and Inspiration; thine, now and always, be the Glory.

There are many people, orders, and groups mentioned in this classic initiatory history lecture, but there are a few of particular interest.

The Knights Templar

Shortly after the first Christian crusade, five years of bloodshed that ended in A.D. 1099, a French knight named Hugues de Payens and several countrymen journeyed to Jerusalem, there establishing a group of religious warrior–mystics. They called this group the "Order of Poor Fellow Soldiers of Christ and the Temple of Solomon," later shortened to simply "Order of the Temple of Jerusalem." This order came to be popularly known as the Knights Templar. This small group of monks took vows of obedience, chastity, and poverty, and were charged primarily with protecting Christian pilgrims from thieves and other attackers on the roads to Jerusalem.

Eventually, this small group became the most powerful military and trade presence in the Holy Land. Their monastic rule allowed them neither to ask for or grant quarter, nor did it allow them to be ransomed if captured. It forbade them from retreating from battle unless the enemy number was at least three times greater than their own. They seemingly had no fear of death, and were grim combatants in their holy cause. Soon, these white-robed, bearded knights were feared throughout the Christian world for their military might upon land and sea, their political power and, perhaps most of all, for their massive treasuries. On their shoulder and breast, they wore a red cross, now known as the Templar Cross.

This eight-pointed (more properly, eight-cornered) geometric figure was used by the Templars as sign and symbol of their own aspirations for regeneration and rebirth. For each knight was reborn into the order upon reception and initiation, never again to be the man he was before, but bound by oath and deed to the highest imaginings of the Christian god and logos. To this day, a form of this same red cross that adorned each knight in battle is seen in areas of strife and battle throughout the world as the emblem of the International Red Cross.

From whence came their strength in battle? Whatever might befall a Templar in life, in battle, or in worship, he knew death was neither a mystery nor to be feared, but rather a fulfillment of life, a natural and necessary return in the cycle of the endless upward spiral of the approach to light. What men called death was no death to the wise, but merely a frightening fairytale told to children. This was the true secret treasure of the Templar.

The Knights Templar are not directly within the lineage of Aurum Solis, but their wisdom and symbolism were drawn from the same sources, a parallel tradition in Ogdoadic history. The Knights are another corner of the Ogdoadic tapestry, quite close to our own, and we draw inspiration and strength from the deep wisdom and great strength of our brothers Templar, for we are each a vital part of this grand tradition.

The Platonic Academy

In mid–15th-century Florence, the Italian *Academia Platonica* met under the leadership of Marsilio Ficino to discuss and trans-

late philosophy and the Greek classics. The inner and most important members of this group were Cosimo and Lorenzo deMedici;
Politian (a.k.a. Poliziano), the outstanding poet and classical
scholar; Cristofero Landino, professor of poetry and oratory at the
University of Florence; and the philosophers Pico della Mirandola
and Gentile deBecchi.

This academy met at the Medici Villa at Careggi, a small town
outside of Florence. They posessed a vast library of Greek manu-
scripts that made the academy one of the foremost intellectual
centers of Renaissance Europe. The awakening that they precipi-
tated in the minds of Europe during their ascendeancy dramatically changed the way we think about philosophy, spirituality,
love, and relationships to this very day.[3] The Medici family, almost
single-handedly, sparked the Italian Renaissance, and the work at
Careggi was instrumental in this. This great influence upon
humanity grew not only from the public works and studies these
men began and explored. The hidden work accomplished in the
inner circle had an even farther-reaching effect upon the minds of
many. Indeed, it profoundly influenced and forever changed the
search for light among the wise and the few. The Careggi Circle was
the circle within which a great current was contacted, focused, and
brought down to the Italian people. Few workings of magick have
equaled this work.

The church strongly objected to the Medici transferring political power in Florence from the papacy to secular rule. On April 26,
1478, Giuliano deMedici was murdered by the Pazzi, a family with
papal backing who attempted to force the Medici from Florence.
This was the first in a series of murders that, over the next two
years, degenerated into virtually open warfare in Florence, resulting in some loss to and much scattering of the Careggi inner circle.

Thus ended the work of the academy. By 1494, after Lorenzo's death, the Medici were expelled from Florence by the French army, but the alchemy begun by the catalyst of their work continues its work even today.

Marsilio Ficino

Highly placed in the text of our history lecture is Marsilio Ficino, a brilliant philosopher and translator of ancient texts who became the first scholar to translate the complete works of Plato into Latin. Ficino was born at 9:00 P.M. on October 19, 1433, at Figline, near Florence. Thus Saturn weighed heavily among his natal planets. Ficino was the son of a successful physician. Perhaps more important, however, is the fact that his mother was a noted clairvoyant who caused great stir among her family, friends, and neighbors with a number of strikingly accurate predictions of future events, including a prediction of her own mother's death, and the time and exact location of her husband's serious fall from a horse.

Ficino was trained in Latin, medicine, Greek, and theology. His father brokered a successful introduction to the Medici for Marsilio and, by 1462, the younger Ficino was living in the Medici household at Careggi and was Master of the Platonic Academy. In 1473, he was ordained a priest and held a position at the Florence cathedral. He completed the first translations of Plato into Latin, along with the works of the Neoplatonic philosopher Plotinus. It is for this that he is most often mentioned in history textbooks. During his time at Careggi, however, Ficino also translated many of the major Hermetic works, bringing forward teachings that might otherwise have been lost, while adding his own insightful commentaries and incorporating many of these teachings in his famous *Book of Life*.

When the Medici were expelled from Florence, Ficino retired to the countryside to continue writing and teaching. He died at Careggi on October 1, 1499.[4]

Angelo Poliziano

Better known among academicians as Politian, this noted scholar was born July 14, 1454, in Tuscany. Around 1469, he was sent to Florence, where he distinguished himself as a scholar with his translatations of Greek and Latin aphorisms and poetry. He caught the attention of Lorenzo deMedici, who invited him to join the Medici household at Careggi in 1473. Here, he was given full access to the considerable resources of the Medici library, and was initiated into the Careggi Circle. Politian and Lorenzo deMedici changed the course of literature in Italy. The poetry of Politian is held to be among the greatest of Italian literary accomplishments. His particular influence on the Careggi work is not known, but it is not hard to imagine how the contributions of a poet of his skill might influence the workings there.[5]

After his work at Careggi, Politian traveled widely, until he was taken under the wing of Cardinal Francesco Gonzaga at Mantua. Here, he wrote *Orpheus*, one of his greatest works. He returned to Florence in 1480 at the invitation of the Medici. Although he had lost his place of favor in the Medici household, he taught and wrote there until he retired. Politian died at the end of September, 1494.

Reuchlin

Johannes Reuchlin was born on February 22, 1455, in Pforzheim, Württemberg (an area in what is now Germany). He was a specialist in the translation and defense of Hebrew literature, and was one of the first German authors to push for the necessity of an education in Greek and Hebrew in order to fully understand Christian scriptures. His academic work was instrumental in creating interest in studying the Christian bible in the original languages, especially Old Testament Hebrew, for which he produced a grammar and lexicon, *De Rudimentis Hebraicis* (The Fundamentals of Hebrew).

It was in his work as a humanist, however, that we most clearly see Reuchlin's inner work and accomplishments. In controversies with the Dominicans of his time, Reuchlin defended Hebrew literature at a time when there was a campaign to burn books written in Hebrew on the principle (espoused by the Dominicans) that Hebrew literature and Judaism were hostile to Christianity.

While his exterior arguments supported the contributions Hebrew literature had made to the development of Christian thought, in less public ways, Reuchlin was preserving a great deal of the Qabalistic writing available in his native land. In 1517, he produced *De Arte Cabbalistica*, one of the first texts to make Qabalah available to non-Jewish readers. This began some of the most important work Reuchlin would do: the creation of a Christian Qabalah, moving Qabalistic thought out of the closed circles of Hebrew scholarship and into a much wider interest group. The occult philosophies of the 16th, 17th, and 18th centuries, and even those of today, are direct outgrowths of the work done by Reuchlin, Pico Della Mirandola, Gilles of Viterbo, and others. Portions of Reuchlin's translation of Hebrew Qabalistic literature into Latin survive even today, copied nearly word for word in numerous English texts on the subject.

Reuchlin died on June 6, 1522, at Bad Liebenzell. He is celebrated as a major figure of the Northern Renaissance who worked a mighty current of change and enlightenment among his people, kindling a light in the north of Europe, much as the Careggi Circle had shed light in the south.

The Order of the Helmet

One Aurum Solis Order document tells us this regarding the Order of the Helmet:

> This society was established in England during the reign of Elizabeth I, and combined Guild, Fideli d'Amore and Careggi successions. It and its members are currently the subject of much academic interest and research. Francis Bacon, Christopher Marlowe and many another notable were among its initiates. Deeply involved with the beginnings of the helmet was the "Italianate" movement of the early years of Elizabeth's reign...
>
> The Order of the Helmet, in its full development surrounding the Mysteries with the new intense feeling of English identity and power which characterized that age, survived well into the 17th century in the person of its initiates.[6]

The Order of the Helmet is mentioned several times in literature, most prominently in the dramatic writing of Francis Bacon, who, in his younger days, was the moving spirit of the order. The Order of the Helmet was a knighthood dedicated to Pallas Athena. In the *Gesta Grayorum* (London, 1688), this order is stated to be guarded by the helmet of the great goddess Pallas. Elsewhere in this work is a passage in which counselors are seen advising a monarch on how to assure that he will be remembered in history. The third counselor, advising buildings and orders as the finest legacy, says:

> Neither do I, excellent Prince, restrain my speeches to dead buildings only, but intend it also to other foundations, institutions, and creations; wherein I presume the more to speak confidently, because I am warranted herein by your own wisdom, who have made the first-fruits of your actions of state to institute the honourable Order of the Helmet; the less shall I need to say, leaving your Excellency not so much to follow my advice as your own example.[7]

Later, the Articles of the Helmet are stated to be:

> Item, Every Knight of this Order shall endeavour to add Conference and Experience by Reading; and therefore shall not only read and peruse Guiza, the French Academy, Galiatto the Courtier, Plutarch, the Arcadia, and the Neoterical Writers from time to time; but also frequent the Theatre, and such like places of Experience and resort to the better sort of Ordinaries for Conference.[8]

Interest in the Order of the Helmet is alive among both scholars studying the life of Bacon and dramaticists who regard Bacon as one of the prime movers in bringing the psychodrama of ancient ritual into modern theater.

Societas Rotae Fulgentis

This group of academics and antiquarians are a vital link in the Ogdoadic tradition. The society used its considerable talent and resources to gather together the history, philosophy, symbolism, and dramatic rituals of several Ogdoadic lines, creating the basis for the great Ogdoadic system we have today. Without the work of these dedicated individuals, there would be no Aurum Solis.

Order documents describe the Societas Rotae Fulgentis as:

> ...the inner body of the antiquarian society from which Aurum Solis was formed. A collation of Ogdoadic teachings and practices was begun as early as 1689, and the tradition was continued under the guise of antiquarianism from the early years of the 18th century...Apart from initiation, the Society of the Blazing Wheel would not seem to have essayed the practical works of Light. While the members were little occupied with these, they were much concerned with their particular duty as they saw it to be: the preservation of the tradition in as whole and entire a condition as they were able to achieve for it.
>
> Around the year 1860, Societas Rotae Fulgentis was transferred from the West of England to London— specifically to the home of the Martin family, 1 St. Paul's Churchyard. From that time it began to explore in depth

the practical aspects of its heritage and was formally constituted as Aurum Solis in 1897.

The Order Aurum Solis

The founders of Aurum Solis were all senior members of the Societas Rotae Fulgentis, much as the founders of the Golden Dawn were all members of the Masonic order Societas Rosicruciana in Anglia. The first head of Aurum Solis was George Stanton, whose leadership allowed the Order to flourish into the 20th century. The order ceased operations for periods during the First and Second World Wars, resuming uninterrupted activities from 1949 to the present. In 1957, a disagreement over the direction of the Order's growth led to a division of Aurum Solis, with a portion leaving to form the Order of the Sacred Word (OSV). In 1971, the Order was unified once again under the Aurum Solis banner.

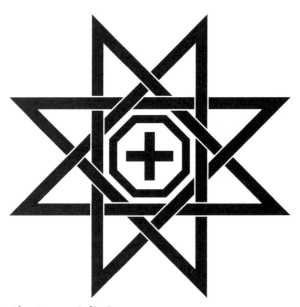

Figure 11. The Aurum Solis Star.

The Aurum Solis Order is active and growing to this day, with a powerful, bright, and vibrant living current. This mighty current is available to those who study independently in our tradition, as well as those who work in our commanderies, temples, and other groups. To study and work with us places the practitioner in some very fine company indeed, and establishes a link to the past, present, and future of this current and the light of our glorious star.

Appendix B:
Recommended
Additional Reading

If you wish to explore some of the material covered in this book more fully or deeply, the following list of titles are recommended to members of the Lapis Lazuli Commandery. Some of the books listed are out of print, but most are easily found in shops dealing in used books. If you have access to the Internet, try searching for old or out-of-print copies of books at one of these sites:

http://www.bibliofind.com   The BiblioFind Webpage
http://www.bookfinder.com   Bookfinder Book Dealer Network

The books listed here are in no particular order, and are certainly not meant to constitute a shopping list for your next trip to the bookstore! I have observed, over the years, that some students have a tendency to confuse the acquisition of books with the acquisition of knowledge. Resist all such ideas. The abilities and accomplishments of a magician are not measured by the size of his or her library.

Browse this list and determine how many, if any, of these books you already have or may have read at some point. If you already have one of them on your bookshelf, start there. Look through these texts and refamiliarize yourself with their contents. As you browse or reread these books, try to look at them from a new point of view: that of the magical way.

For the books you do not already have—and that may be this entire list—make use of the public library or shop at used book stores. Only purchase or borrow books as you need them. There is little point to putting time and energy into assembling a library of magical books you haven't read and may never get around to reading. To make this list manageable and useful, I have used a few selection criteria:

- Only items in English have been listed. Lapis Lazuli reading includes works in other languages, but not at the introductory level.
- The Aurum Solis and Lapis Lazuli documents that constitute much of the reading in the early stages are not listed. These are not generally available to the solitary student, though many are published in the *Magical Philosophy* series. The important ones have been summarized in this book.
- In each section, there were many possible candidates. It is a painful and arbitrary process to trim the many good selections down to a few that best represent each category. I hope that I have succeeded in this. You will be the judge.

Aurum Solis

Foundations of High Magick, Denning and Phillips.
The Sword and the Serpent, Denning and Phillips.
Mysteria Magica, Denning and Phillips.

These books contain the outer documents of the Aurum Solis Order. Unfortunately, they are long out of print. The first volume has been recently republished and, in time, the others will appear as well.

Planetary Magick, Denning and Phillips.
> A very accessible book with Aurum Solis approaches to the field of planetary magick. Excellent reading that can be used by a group as the foundation for a complete magical system.

Magical States of Consciousness, Denning and Phillips.
> This is the Aurum Solis beginner's text on Qabalistic pathworking.

Astral Projection, Denning and Phillips.
> A beginner's text on astral projection. In my opinion the single best purely practical book on the subject.

Entrance to the Magical Qabalah, Denning and Phillips.
> A beginner's text on Qabalah, and Melita Denning's final work before her passing in 1997. An excellent primer on Qabalistic thought and practice in the Aurum Solis tradition.

Psychology and Mind

Obviously, this is only the beginning of a study of this subject. Aurum Solis has also developed its own form of Qabalistic psychology that is taught as part of the 2nd Hall curriculum.

There is a strong undercurrent of art and dance in Aurum Solis thought and practice. Otto Rank's work is outstanding in understanding this artistic impulse in ourselves from a psychological standpoint. The value of C. G. Jung to the magician cannot be overstated.

Roberto Assaglioli, M.D., *The Act of Will.*

Murry Hope, *The Psychology of Ritual.*

Carl G. Jung, *Psychology and Alchemy.*

Carl G. Jung, *Structure and Dynamics of the Psyche.*

Carl G. Jung, *Mysterium Coniunxionis.*

Carl G. Jung, *Alchemical Studies.*

Otto Rank, *The Myth of the Birth of the Hero.*

Otto Rank, *Art and Artist.*

Western Magick

Obviously, there are thousands of books available on this topic. In addition to the Aurum Solis books listed above, these books have proven useful, or at least interesting, to many students. Working through these introductory texts, you will undoubtedly find the desire to explore certain authors more fully.

Aleister Crowley, *Magick.*

A landmark work in the field, though it may be difficult reading for the beginner. Be sure to keep your sense of humor handy and try not to take Crowley too seriously.

Lon Milo Duquette, *The Magick of Thelema.*

Duquette is a Crowley apologist, and a very good one. He has written an entertaining and comprehensible introduction to the rituals and magick of the Ordo Templi Orientis.

Dion Fortune, *Cosmic Doctrine.*

This book represents the foundation of Fortune's teachings.

Dion Fortune, *Esoteric Orders and Their Work.*

This was once required introductory reading in Dion Fortune's society. A brief and good introduction to the history of Western magick from the English point of view.

David Godwin, *Light in Extension.*

One of the few books to examine the contributions of Greek magick and thought to modern magical thinking. This book is very useful to any Aurum Solis student.

William Gray, *Attainment Through Magic.*

Gray's book is an introduction to a system of magick descended from Dion Fortune. This book is an excellent discussion of magick that delves deeply into the "why" of magick, as well as the "how."

Donald Michael Kraig, *Modern Magick.*

An excellent introductory text to any practice of magick, with a particular emphasis on the Golden Dawn approach. Highly recommended.

Symbolism of Attainment

These books represent different viewpoints on the spiritual ideal, and what we might find at the end of the path. St. John of the Cross is exceptional reading and should be considered essential.

Rubaiyat of Omar Khayyam, any edition.
The Holy Books of Thelema, Aleister Crowley.
The Living Flame of Love and its Commentary, St. John of the Cross.
"On a dark night" (poem), St. John of the Cross.

The last two works can be found in any edition of *The Collected Works of Saint John of the Cross* by Kavanaugh and Rodriguez. This soft-cover book is difficult to find, but well worth the trouble.

Historical and Philosophical Background

Mortimer Adler, *Aristotle for Everybody.*

Aristotle can be challenging reading. Adler helps readers new to Aristotle understand the core of his system. Highly recommended.

Aristotle, *The Nichomachean Ethics.*

One of the more complete presentations of Aristotlian thought.

E. A. Wallis Budge, *Gods of the Egyptians* and *The Egyptian Book of the Dead.*

These books form the basis of much of the Egyptian magick found in the modern world. They are somewhat dated and contain some mistakes, but are still respected.

Franz Cumont, *Astrology and Religion Among the Greeks and Romans.*

An interesting work, somewhat specialized.

Marsilio Ficino, as translated by Charles Boer, *Book of Life.*

Essential book for understanding the roots of Aurum Solis and the environment and thinking of the Italian Rennaisance.

W. K. Guthrie, *The Greeks and Their Gods.*

A solid introductory work on early Greek religious thought

Herodotus, *The Histories.*

Essential reading for an understanding of the Greek world. Herodotus is the father of modern history.

Plato, *The Republic* and *Crito, Phaedo, Ion and Meno* (dialogues).

These are the dialogues of Plato essential to understanding his philosophical system.

Plotinus, *The Enneads.*

Plotinus is a good representative of Neoplatonic thought, heavily influenced by the Gnostics. His thought is very much a part of the ideas from which Aurum Solis was eventually born.

There is a good and inexpensive paperback edition published by Penguin.

Poetry

Poetry is such a broad field, with so many offerings, that I was forced to use some very narrow criteria in preparing this section, which is entirely biased toward my favorites or poets from whom I have frequently borrowed in the creation of rites. All of these authors are writing, at least symbolically, about the path of light. Most of them were members of esoteric orders. All of them have some bearing on Aurum Solis teaching and practice. All wrote originally in English, a choice I made to reduce the problems that arise when reading translations, although several French, Spanish, and Arabic poets are brilliant in their explorations of the indwelling divine.

Collected Poems of W.B. Yeats,

> particularly "The Rose," "The Tower," "The Wanderings of Oisin," "The Old Age of Queen Maeve," "Baile and Aillinn," "The Shadowy Waters," "The Two Kings," and "The Gift of Harun Al-Rashid." Yeats was the head of the Golden Dawn for a time and his writings clearly show his progression from Candidate to Adept. All of his writings are important to the Western esoteric traditions, but those listed above are some of the most directly applicable.

William Blake, *Songs of Innocence and Experience* and *The Rossetti Manuscript.*

> Blake is the poet who has inspired perhaps more magical poetry than any other. Foundational works, these can be difficult reading, but are worth the effort.

Edward Carpenter, *The Drama of Love and Death* and *Towards Democracy.*

Carpenter is a poet and student of human nature who wrote a number of groundbreaking books in the early part of the 20th century. His master work, *Towards Democracy,* contains some of the most beautiful lines written concerning the path to attainment and the achievement of the light. His work should be required reading for every serious magician. His poetry is eminently suitable for adaptation to magical rites.

T. S. Eliot, *Journey of the Magi* and *Two Choruses from The Rock.*

A man with no small involvement in esoteric matters himself, T. S. Eliot wrote the above works from the perspective of a tradition very close to our own. Parts of *The Rock* are used in a Lapis Lazuli celebration of Winter Solstice.

John Keats—Any poetry of.

Not easy reading generally, but the symbolism of John Keats is alchemical in nature and can be very useful.

Reference

Any large dictionary of English will do for a start, even a paperback.

A good Latin dictionary is essential. There are many of these in used bookstores. Find one that seems well organized and keep it on hand. Avoid dictionaries specialized toward medicine or law, but those including Roman Catholic church Latin are very useful.

A good Greek dictionary is important, but may be and somewhat difficult to find. Look in used bookstores, and be sure that the dictionary covers classical, not modern, Greek.

Aleister Crowley, *777*.

This is a basic work on Qabalistic correspondences and gematria, in the style of the Golden Dawn. Numerology is much less emphasized in the Aurum Solis tradition than in the Crowley-based traditions, but a familiarity with the basic technique is necessary.

Antonia Frazier, *The Golden Bough*.

This is an important collection of folktales and myths from around the world. Very useful in the development of rites and highly recommended.

David Godwin, *Godwin's Cabalistic Encyclopedia*.

For many years, *777* was the standard for tables of Qabalistic correspondences. David Godwin's work is excellent, comprehensive, and filled with information that goes far beyond *777*, or anything else available in previous years.

Sir William Smith, *Smaller Classical Dictionary*.

You will want a good classical dictionary. This one, available in paperback and often seen in used bookstores, is an inexpensive starter reference that should see you through the first year or so of study. Very useful, and still the one I use most often.

AURUM SOLIS: ORDER OF THE SACRED WORLD

If you want to continue your study of Aurum Solis Art Magick, you should first try to locate an Aurum Solis Commandery, temple, or study group in your area. Unfortunately, such groups are few and far between. The names, descriptions, and contact information of those Commanderies, daughter temples, and sanctioned study groups that wish to be publicly known may be found on the Aurum Solis website at

http://www.aurumsolis.org

The Aurum Solis mailing address is:
Administrator-General,
Grand Commandery of Aurum Solis,
BM Stargate, London WCIN 3XX
ENGLAND
E-mail: Athlit@aurumsolis.org

If you cannot find an Aurum Solis group in your area, consider starting a study group of your own. After all, that is what Marsilio Ficino, Cosimo and Lorenzo deMedici, Politian, and Pico della Mirandola did when they formed the Platonic Academy. Otherwise, persevere, and remember that group study is not superior to solitary study and practice. In fact, very few of the great adepts and magicians of history developed their skills in a group environment.

ENDNOTES

INTRODUCTION

1. Swami Vivikenanda, *Raji Yoga* (Calcutta: Advaita Ashrama, 1973), preface.

2. Quotations are from Aurum Solis Order papers and other documents. Many of these were published in four volumes by Denning & Phillips: *Mysteria Magica*, St. Paul, MN: Llewellyn, 1988; *Planetary Magic*, St. Paul, MN: Llewellyn, 1989; *The Foundations of High Magick*, St. Paul, MN: Llewellyn, 1991; and *The Sword and the Serpent*, St. Paul, MN: Llewellyn, 1992. Quotations from these works, used by permission of the publisher. Quotations from unpublished Aurum Solis papers used by permission of the Grand Master of the Order.

CHAPTER ONE

1. Melita Denning and Osborne Phillips, *Foundations of High Magick* (St. Paul, MN: Llewellyn), p. xviii.

2. Murry Hope, *Practical Greek Magic* (London: Aquarian Press, 1985), introduction.

3. Eliphas Levi, *Transcendental Magic* (York Beach, ME: Weiser Books, 1974), note on p. 12.

4. Aleister Crowley, *Magick* (London: Arkana, 1989), p. 131.

5. Crowley, *Magick*, p. 132.

6. Once in a while, I meet someone in the magical community who declares that there are no longer any secrets in magick. My response to this is always the same: Those who say this never had any secrets in the first place. The great orders are not free with their hard-gained and powerful hidden knowledge. Silence is the very thing that gives these secrets power. Who, having gained such hard-earned mysteries, would then disempower them by betraying their oaths? In a less esoteric vein, it is a philosophical and logical truth that one can never prove that something does *not* exist, only that it does, and then only upon evidence.

Chapter Two

1. T. S. Eliot, *The Waste Land and Other Poems* (New York: Harcourt, Brace & World, 1962), p. 87.

2. Quoted in Eknath Easwaran, *The Upanishads* (Tomales: Nilgiri Press, 1987), p. 205.

3. Easwaran, *Upanishads*, p. 209–210.

Chapter Three

1. Though most such writers have discoverd at one time or another that someone around them acts in a way contrary to

their personal sense of right and wrong, thereby acting with the very ethics they deny. After all, to call the police when you have been robbed is an act of ethical judgment.

2. Aleister Crowley, *Magick Without Tears* (Phoenix, AZ: Falcon, 1987), p. 424.

3. A grand idea that works well on a cosmic scale, but fails miserably in the everyday life of the microcosm.

4. And "Karma will get him" is not an improvement on "God will get him."

5. Sexual infidelity in marriage, for example. Infidelity is a dishonest manipulation of another. The inconstant one fears that an informed spouse may make some unpleasant decisions about their married life, so the act is kept hidden. This deprives the spouse of her or his right to live life as she or he desires, and is, in every classical definition, pure black magick. "Do as thou wilt," but all such actions do come with an eventual price. The energy it takes to keep such deceptions alive takes away from the energy needed for magical work. Honesty, though the more difficult choice, restores the situation and places responsibility for our own actions squarely where it belongs.

6. Mouni Sadhu, *The Tarot* (Los Angeles: Wilshire Book Company, 1976), p. 166.

7. This premise states that all magical energy sent out returns to us with three times as much energy. It is usually stated only in the negative: evil or dark acts of magick return three times as much harm and evil to the practitioner. Even if it were the case that "black" or "evil" actions were returned three times over, even over the course of several incarnations, basic physics still applies. This leaves us with only two methods for obtaining

the energy for this multiplication of action: either "white" or "good" actions require three times more effort than they produce, or the cosmos is steadily being drained of magical energy.

8. It is from this that the Threefold Law arose, for magical rebounds like these feel *at least* three times worse than you thought they would be. Rebounds result from attempts to heal and other more altruistic motives as well, but these feel rather more benign.

9. Carl Glick, *The Secret of Serenity* (London: Rider and Company), pp. 63–65.

10. Aleister Crowley, *Magick Without Tears*, p. 311.

11. An example of this principle may be seen in an interesting and ironic occurrence in America in the 1960s as Hitler's car, the Volkswagen, carried so many American hippies to antiwar, propeace rallies, raising America's consciousness about war, and forever changing this country's policies about military engagement. Magick, as life, is never simple.

12. See Dion Fortune's novels *The Sea Priestess* and *Moon Magic* for excellent examples of this process on a grand scale.

13. Exceptions may exist, of course, but let us set these aside for the sake of discussion and assume that we are talking about a person who has done no heinous act.

14. Dion Fortune, *Sane Occultism* (London: Aquarian Press, 1967), p. 144.

15. A. J. Arberry, trans., *Discourses of Rumi* (York Beach, ME: Weiser Books, 1972), p. 61.

CHAPTER FOUR

1. The Chamber of Art will be many things to you over time, but, ultimately, the adept finds that the true Chamber of Art is one's own body, the dwelling place of the divine. Until that realization comes in full measure, we are each our own priest and priestess, and we need an appropriate temple for our work.

CHAPTER FIVE

1. Edward Carpenter, *Pagan and Christian Creeds* (New York: Harcourt, Brace & Howe, 1920), p. 239.
2. Members of the Lapis Lazuli Commandery are well aware of this principle and will recognize the method.
3. In a later work, we will explore this technique more fully.
4. Simply note these dreams, do not become overconcerned with their analysis. The meaning of many dreams will become apparent only over time, and the meaning of others will change over time.
5. People always enjoy receiving invitations to such things as a Winter Solstice Party, at which the hosts may set the tone for the evening by lighting the scene only with candles, small lights, or other symbolic reminders of the theme of this day: light in the midst of darkness.
6. Edward Carpenter, *A Visit to Gnani* (London: George Allen & Co., 1911), p. 65. There are many such books available, but classics such as those by Dion Fortune are excellent.
7. As a general rule, I have found that those who own the most books are the ones most likely to have "skimmed" a great deal.

8. This is a difficult lesson, for our culture teaches us the opposite: a great breadth of superficial knowledge is held to be quite impressive, though its usefulness appears to be aimed primarily at cocktail parties.

9. Occasionally, a student may wish to use a computer for the magical diary. I advise against this, on two grounds: First, the computer forces you to compose your diary almost entirely in text. The value of the diary, however, is not merely the text you write, but also the pictures you draw, the diagrams you create, the line with an arrow drawn between two sentences that links them in a new and important manner. Much is lost when we turn the art of the diary into the task of word processing. Second, a computer, with its abstract keyboard and various technical aspects that must be borne in mind, draws us stongly to our "left-brain," analytical self, reducing input from the "right-brain," artistic self.

10. These may be readily obtained in many New Age shops, especially those with a "Gothic" effect, and at Renaissance fairs.

11. The ring may be placed on any finger, though it may take some time to understand the significance of each particular finger. Many, following magicians of old, place the ring on the index finger of the right hand, symbolizing power and authority over spirits and energies. Others place it on the ring finger of the right hand, symbolizing a commitment to the way of light stronger and more lasting than Earthly marriage.

12. From an Aurum Solis document.

CHAPTER SIX

1. Marsilio Ficino, *Book of Life* (Woodstock, CT: Spring Publications, 1994), p. 17.
2. Yogi Ramacharaka, *Science of Breath* (Yogi Publication Society, 1904), p. 8.
3. Ramacharaka, *Science of Breath*, p. 20.
4. Swami Vivekananda, *Raja Yoga* (Calcutta: Advaita Ashrama, 1973), p. 62.
5. Claude Larre, *The Secret Treatise of the Spiritual Orchid* (Cambridge: Monkey Press, 1992).
6. Swami Vivekananda, *Raja Yoga*, p. 92.

CHAPTER SEVEN

1. Joseph Campbell, *Hero With a Thousand Faces* (Princeton: Bollingen, 1973).
2. The concepts of Jung's unconcious and Freud's subconcious are often confused. Jung's idea of the universal unconcious is that of a culturally shared storehouse of images, experiences, and archetypes that flow *into* the mind. Freud's subconcious is a storehouse of experiences and images from our minds that have been pushed down, away from normal conciousness. We may be aware of our subconcious and bring our own personal demons from it into the light of concious thought, but the unconcious is only available to those who study and doggedly pursue the mysteries.
3. C. G. Jung. *The Portable Jung* (New York: Viking Press, 1971), p. 161.

4. Christopher Vogler, *The Writer's Journey* (Studio City: Michael Wiese Productions, 1998).

5. Volger, *Writer's Journey*, p. 74.

6. Nancy Watson, *Practical Solitary Magic* (York Beach: Weiser Books, 1996), p. 154.

CHAPTER EIGHT

1. "Be gone, afar, unholy ones": a powerful and ancient banishing charge that, due to its effectiveness, has endured through both classical and modern times.

CHAPTER NINE

1. Marion Zimmer Bradley, *Mists of Avalon* (New York: Ballantine Books, 1982), p. 198.

2. Ibid.

3. Nancy Watson, *Practical Solitary Magic* (York Beach, ME: Samuel Weiser, 1996), p. 47.

4. Fortunately, you'll not be attempting anything of that duration. Even among advanced magicians and adepts, there are few who can maintain focus in a rite for that long. Moreover, the need would have to be something more than mere speculation about the outcome.

5. People often forget that psychic and magical work can be every bit as tiring as hard physical labor, depending on the nature of the rite.

CHAPTER TEN

1. A game with some value to the study of magick, as we will see when we later approach the topic of divination.

2. And of no less value to the student of Eastern traditions!

3. As the student advances and begins the study of the planets and the zodiac, it is easy to lose touch with the knowledge gained through experiences with the four elements. To do so, however, is to render impotent the weapons, to deny oneself contact with the elementals, and, most dangerous indeed, to lose the firm grounding from which we reach out and within. To lose contact and practice with the elements is to forget nature. Whatever other glamorous or spiritual things we may be, we are, from the moment of birth, a part of nature.

4. There is a magical concept of great importance within this sentence. More classically stated, this is the principle, "As above, so below."

5. Put another way, electricians and plumbers are both called to work during the building of a new house, and at about the same stage of the building process. Yet this experience does not give either more than a superficial understanding of the other's craft.

6. This result is of no less value to us: one's understanding of an element is greatly advanced by interaction with one of these denizens of the elemental worlds.

7. And, of course, we all have the good sense to put on a raincoat before "braving the elements."

8. From an Aurum Solis document.

9. From an Aurum Solis document.

10. Psalms 22:14.

11. Author's translation.

12. From an Aurum Solis document.

13. From the perspective of any one location on Earth.

14. It has not been unusual in the course of history for elementals to be mistaken for gods.

15. From an Aurum Solis document.

16. It is interesting to note the elemental nature of our traditional rites of burial. We bury the dead in earth; we cremate the dead in fire; we spread cremated ashes upon the air; we bury the dead in seas of water.

17. Not spirit dominated by nature, as some would describe it, leading to much of the fear and misunderstanding in our world that springs forth at each appearance of an "upside-down" pentagram.

18. Katherine Kurtz, *The Adept Book Two: The Lodge of the Lynx* (New York: Ace Books, 1992), p. 345.

19. From an Aurum Solis document.

20. A word from old French, meaning "life."

21. Ficino, *Book of Life* (Woodstock, CT: Spring Publications, 1994), p. 191.

CHAPTER ELEVEN

1. Likewise, if you skip past the previous work, you will find the shortcomings of your study here as well.

2. In fact, you would one day come to the knowledge necessary for so many things: that what is to be learned is found in the one moment that the cup is immersed in water, or any other total moment of the present during the action. There is an old say-

ing from the East that is often true of the study of magick: "The more talking and thinking, the farther from the truth."

3. An idea not markedly different from the Taoist concept of creation.

4. "Imagined" is not a word by which to dismiss concepts, for it is simply a word denoting the creation of an image in the mind. Most of the great discoveries of modern science rest on the "imaginings" of scientists. Imagination is just one valid tool of investigation and discovery.

5. From an Aurum Solis document.

6. Charles Ponce, *Kabbalah* (Wheaton, IL: Quest Books, 1978), p. 93.

7. From lecture notes.

8. Author's own translation from Chinese.

9. J. Abelson, *Jewish Mysticism* (London: G. Bell & Sons, 1913), p. 137.

10. W. Wescott, ed., *Sepher Yetzirah* (New York: Occult Research Press), pp. 15–17.

11. This is by no means the only arrangement of the sephiroth and paths. Although this is the most prevalent model of the Tree of Life, keep in mind that it is nothing more than a model through which we may enjoy one particular view of these mysteries. Other arrangements reveal other wisdom, and Qabalistic mysticism posits many such models.

12. This is one way we use tarot, which is generally designed with these purposes in mind. When tarot is used only as a vehicle of divination, the potential of these powerful images is limited to the material world. Tarot covers a much wider scope, where the truth and beauty of magick come to life in the dreamlike imagery of the tarot.

Chapter Twelve

1. Start with written records, however. This practice requires discipline and precision to gain the magical tools sought. On-the-fly mental reviews lack this precision.

Chapter Thirteen

1. Aleister Crowley, *Magick* (York Beach, ME: Weiser Books, 1989), p. 132.
2. By this, I do not intend to perpetuate the oft-stated idea that magick is science or scientific. While some tools of science are useful to the magician, such as record keeping and objective experimentation, magick is not a science and magicians are not scientists. Like engineers, we apply science in a practical manner. Like craftspeople, we often rely on acquired skill more than learning. In ritual, we occasionally create works of true art. Magicians are artisans, drawing from the best of every part of what we have seen, and learned, and dreamt.

Chapter Fourteen

1. Fall brings the Harvest Moon that shines for one night longer than other Full Moons of the year.
2. Actually, 70 minutes and 20 seconds, but, for most calculations, one may round to the lower number and simply start a rite in the midst of the desired magical hour, leaving room for a few minutes of error.

CHAPTER FIFTEEN

1. Ficino, *Book of Life* (Woodstock, CT: Spring Publications, 1994), p. 73.

APPENDIX A

1. Paul Foster Case, *The Tarot* (Richmond: Macoy Publishing Company, 1975), p. 12.
2. From an Aurum Solis Order document
3. The academy was responsible for postulating and popularizing the concept of Platonic love, which taught that the highest form of love is one based ultimately on the soul's love for God. This began a shift in European thought from love as a matter of property and animal passions to the romantic and spiritual love we embrace and aspire toward in human relationships today.
4. For an excellent, if irreverent, account of Ficino's life and the work of the Platonic Academy, see Ficino's *Book of Life* (Woodstock, CT: Spring Publications, 1996), translated by Charles Boer.
5. I count myself fortunate indeed to have had this very sort of input from one of the members of Lapis Lazuli, himself a true poet of noted accomplishments.
6. From an Aurum Solis document.
7. These quotes are part of the text published by Paul Dupuy via the world wide web at http://fly.hiwaay.net/~paul/outline.html
8. Ibid.

BIBLIOGRAPHY

Assagioli, Roberto. *The Act of Will*. New York: Arkana, 1992.

Carpenter, Edward. *A Visit to a Gnani*. London: George Allen, 1911.

———*Common Sense About Christian Ethics*. New York: Macmillan Company, 1962.

———*The Drama of Love and Death*. London: Mitchell Kennerley, 1912.

———*Pagan and Christian Creeds*. New York: Harcourt, Brace and Howe, 1920.

———*Towards Democracy*. London: Mitchell Kennerley, 1922.

Case, Paul Foster. *The Tarot*. Richmond, VA: Macoy, 1975.

Connelly, Dianne. *Traditional Acupuncture: The Law of the Five Elements*. Columbia, MD: Center for Traditional Acupuncture, 1979.

Crowley, Aleister. *Magick*. London: Arkana, 1973.

———*Magick Without Tears*. Phoenix, AZ: New Falcon, 1987.

Curott, Phyllis. *Book of Shadows*. New York: Broadway Books, 1998.

David-Neel, Alexandra. *Magic and Mystery in Tibet*. New York: Dover, 1971.

Denning and Phillips. *Astral Projection.* St. Paul, MN: Llewellyn, 1994.

———*Creative Visualization.* St. Paul, MN: Llewellyn, 1994.

———*Development of Psychic Powers.* St. Paul, MN: Llewellyn, 1989.

———*Entrance to the Magical Qabalah.* Loughborough, UK: Thoth Publications, 1997.

———*The Foundations of High Magick.* St. Paul, MN: Llewellyn, 1991.

———*Magical States of Consciousness.* St. Paul, MN: Llewellyn, 1988.

———*The Magick of Sex.* St. Paul, MN: Llewellyn, 1982.

———*The Magick of the Tarot.* St. Paul, MN: Llewellyn, 1993.

———*Mysteria Magica.* St. Paul, MN: Llewellyn, 1988.

———*Planetary Magick.* St. Paul, MN: Llewellyn, 1989.

———*The Sword and the Serpent.* St. Paul, MN: Llewellyn, 1992.

Easwaran, Eknath. *The Upanishads.* Tomales: Nilgiri Press, 1987.

Ficino, Marsilio. *Book of Life.* Charles Boer, ed. and tr. Woodstock, CT: Spring, 1994.

Fortune, Dion. *Applied Magic.* York Beach, ME: Weiser Books, 2000.

———*Esoteric Orders and Their Work.* London: Aquarian, 1987.

———*Machinery of the Mind.* York Beach, ME: Samuel Weiser, 1980.

———*The Mystical Qabalah.* York Beach, ME: Samuel Weiser, 1984.

———*Psychic Self Defense.* York Beach, ME: Samuel Weiser, 1992.

———*Sane Occultism.* London: Aquarian Press, 1967.

Galen. *On the Natural Faculties.* Arthur John Brock, ed. and tr. Cambridge, MA: Harvard University Press, 1963.

Glick, Carl. *The Secret of Serenity.* London: Rider, 1953.

Godwin, David. *The Cabalistic Encyclopedia*. St. Paul, MN: Llewellyn, 1994.

———*Light in Extension*. St. Paul, MN: Llewellyn, 1992.

Gray, William. *Attainment Through Magic*. St. Paul, MN: Llewellyn, 1990.

———*Between Good and Evil*. St. Paul, MN: Llewellyn, 1989.

———*Temple Magic*. St. Paul, MN: Llewellyn, 1988.

Hall, Manly. *Unseen Forces*. Los Angeles: Hall Publishing, 1929.

Hope, Murry. *The Greek Tradition*. Shaftesbury, UK: Element Books, 1989.

———*The Psychology of Ritual*. Shaftesbury, UK: Element Books, 1988.

Jung, Carl, ed. *Man and His Symbols*. New York: Dell Publishing, 1968.

———*The Portable Jung*. Joseph Campbell, ed. New York: Viking Press, 1971.

———*Psyche and Symbol*. Violet S. de Laszlo, ed. New York: Anchor, 1958.

———*The Undiscovered Self*. New York: Mentor Books, 1958.

Kraig, Donald Michael. *Modern Magick*. St. Paul, MN: Llewellyn, 1990.

Larre, Claude and Elisabeth Rochat de la Vallee. *The Secret Treatise of the Spiritual Orchid*. Cambridge, UK: Monkey Press, 1992.

———*The Way of Heaven*. Cambridge, UK: Monkey Press, 1994.

Levi, Eliphas. *Transcendental Magic*. York Beach, ME: Samuel Weiser, 1974.

Plotinus. *The Enneads*. London: Penguin Books, 1991.

Ponce, Charles. *The Game of Wizards*. Wheaton, IL: Quest Books, 1973.

———*Kabbalah*. Wheaton, IL: Quest Books, 1978.

Ramaharaka, Yogi. *Science of Breath*. Chicago: Yogi Publication Society, 1905.

Reuchlin, Johann. *On the Art of the Kabbalah*. Sarah Goodman, ed. Martin and tr. Lincoln, NE: University of Nebraska Press, 1993.

Richardson, Alan. *The Magical Life of Dion Fortune*. London: Aquarian, 1991.

Sadhu, Mouni. *The Tarot*. Hollywood, CA: Wilshire, 1976.

Shrine of Wisdom. *The Divine Pymander*. Fintry, Brook, UK: The Shrine of Wisdom, 1970.

Vivekananda, Swami. *Raja Yoga*. Calcutta: Advaita Ashrama, 1973.

Vogler, Christopher. *The Writer's Journey*. Studio City, CA: Michael Wiese, 1998.

Wang, Robert. *Qabalistic Tarot*. York Beach, ME: Samuel Weiser, 1987.

Watson, Nancy. *Practical Solitary Magic*. York Beach, ME: Samuel Weiser, 1996.

Wilhelm, Richard. *The I Ching*. Cary Baynes, tr. Princeton: Princeton University Press, 1961.

INDEX